TABLE OF CONTENTS

Prologue   1

Chapter 1: Vic is Dead   5

Chapter 2: Viva la Huelga!   27

Chapter 3: The Movement: 1969-70   51

Chapter 4: Decision Time   77

Chapter 5: Into the Resistance   99

Chapter 6: Mayday! Mayday! May 1, 1971   130

Chapter 7: Disillusioned Disciple   169

Chapter 8: Another Kind of Commitment   194

Epilogue   209

PROLOGUE

We pushed through the rear doors of the auditorium and marched straight into the business meeting of the Missouri District of the Lutheran Church (Missouri Synod), down the center aisle toward the stage, 23 pairs of hands clapping, our voices raised in song:

> "...*Gonna lay down my sword and shield*
>
> *Down by the riverside*
>
> *Ain't gonna study war no more...*"

It was Tuesday, June 17, 1970: my eighteenth birthday. I wanted the several hundred church leaders there to know I would not register for the draft that day, even though it was required by law when men turned 18. I was resisting the draft after more than a year of organizing war protests in high school, wrestling with my conscience, and arguing with my parents. I wanted the leaders to support me by taking a public stand against the draft and the war in Vietnam, a war that had just been drastically escalated and expanded the month before with the U.S. invasion of Cambodia.

My friends and I—all members of Lutheran youth groups, such as Black Youth Unlimited, the Walther League or the St. Louis Hunger Team—had attended the Missouri District's meetings all week to engage our church's leaders in polite discussions about hunger, racism, and the war. Today was different. Today we were done talking. We wanted action. We stopped the meeting and took the stage to make our point.

I never thought they would let us on the stage, let alone leave the podium microphone on, so I had not planned to say anything—-just march, clap, and sing. But now, we stopped singing, and silence filled the auditorium. Feeling woozy but having no choice, I stepped up to the podium.

I grabbed the smooth sides of the podium, looking over the crowd, and—in a shaky voice cracking with emotion—talked about how wrong the war was, and how Martin Luther taught us to follow our consciences. Stiff-lipped, glaring men greeted my words with silent hostility. A short, old man stood off to the side, hunched over his cane but looking intensely at me while talking to the equally ancient woman standing next to him. Her eyes were glued to me as she shook her head. These two were my Great Aunt Liode and Great Uncle Arthur, a Lutheran pastor who had served a congregation in the north St. Louis neighborhood of Baden for more than 50 years. He was long since retired, and both were in their mid-80s.

As I spoke, they turned away and hobbled out the same door my friends and I had marched through. I was not particularly close to Uncle Arthur and Aunt Liode, but I *had* spoken with them earlier in the week, and they had been very friendly. Why were they leaving? I mentally shrugged it off and finished my speech. Then, we took up our singing and clapping again and made our way back out of the auditorium. Relief and elation washed over me as we walked into the summer morning.

I didn't see my aunt and uncle ever again; they both died within the next few years. I never had the chance to ask them why they walked out while I was speaking. It turns out I wasn't the first Kuehnert family member to publicly protest the draft during an unpopular war: Great Uncle Arthur's brother Paul had resisted during World War I. It strikes me that as Arthur and Liode walked out on me in 1970 they may have been reacting, in part, to memories of 1917 and how that Paul's protest put him—and the extended family—in great jeopardy during another time of great discord\.

I discovered Great Uncle Paul's stand when I found a copy of his World War I draft registration form online. On June 5, 1917, the first mandatory draft registration day in the United States since the Civil War, he had taken his own stand against the draft and the U.S. entry into World War I by writing "conscience against conscription" on his draft registration. To my surprise, I found further records that showed that same uncle was drafted into the Army that September. In less than three months, he had been drafted by the very system he objected to—and in another six, he was being shipped to France to fight. I can only imagine the sleepless nights and soulful internal struggles he experienced, likely for the rest of his life.

I was mystified by these discoveries. Why had Uncle Paul made his conscientious objection to the war and the draft known to the draft board in his small, rural, Missouri town, and then turned around and served in the Army—in combat and wounded? What exactly had happened to and with my uncle from 1917 to 1919? What were the circumstances—in his family, in his small town, in his own conscience—that led to his decision? And why had no one in the family ever talked about all of this or added stories of his protest and his service to the family lore?

As I researched Great Uncle Paul and World War I, I realized that my own story of draft resistance was also a complicated one. Unlike most of my peers who pledged not to register, I reversed my decision and registered for the draft about 18 months after that morning in the seminary auditorium. I was never prosecuted for not registering, and I was not drafted.

I believed then—and now–that I had done these contradictory things out of the same motivation: To find the most effective way to stop a war I thought was wrong in every way. I grew to believe that individual acts of conscience were the starting point—not the ending point— of effective social change. I began to challenge my own assumptions and to understand the limits of my courage in the face of a powerful, adaptive, and complex society. During those tumultuous 18 months in my young life, I was struggling to define myself, find my purpose in life, and connect myself with a community that would support my growth.

And now, fifty years later—living once again through times of great division, moral outrage, and protest actions taken by hundreds of thousands of ordinary Americans—I recall those moments on the stage with a mixture of pride and wonder. I am proud that I took a bold, personal stand against an unjust war. And I marvel at my youthful willingness to risk my future based on faith that my act would make a difference.

Join me as I look back at my journey into "the resistance," and what happened along the way.

Paul Kuehnert

December 2020

CHAPTER 1:
VIC IS DEAD

As I left homeroom and joined the surge of students in the hall, I heard a voice calling my name: "Paul, *Paul*, PAUL!" I looked down the hallway and saw a chunky guy with glasses motioning to me with the hand that was not holding a load of books. It was Steve Musko, once my closest friend and now pretty much a stranger, a varsity football lineman and a part of the jock crowd that I had nothing but contempt for.

I glanced briefly over to my friend Tim, who had followed me out of homeroom, and jerked my head in Steve's direction. "I have to go see what this guy wants. I'll catch up with you." Tim nodded and went on his way. Steve was now about 15 feet away and he said, "Come on, man, I have to tell you something important. Pick it up!"

I pushed my way through the crowd and stood in front of him, the flow of students eddying around us. I was considering some sort of smart-assed comment when I looked into his face and saw his mouth in a tight grimace and his eyes welling up. "It's Vic," he blurted, then continued in a trembling voice. "Vic. Dead. Over there. Fucking stepped on a mine or some shit like that, I don't know. But Vic is dead." He took a deep breath, sighed, and continued: "I thought you should know and you probably didn't. I ran into Renee and her Mom last night. It just happened, like, last week or something …"

"Vic? Vic? Jesus," I croaked and stopped. Vic was one of the neighborhood kids. Although he was older than we were by a couple of years, we had spent countless hours with Vic over the years.

Steve's eyes searched my face. He turned his head and looked over his shoulder, taking in the thinning crowd as the last few students were now scurrying to beat the bell marking the start of the first class period of the day. I stared into the same space over his shoulder, saying nothing. "Look, man, I'm sorry," Steve said, "but I had to find you and let you know. It sucks. I guess I better get to class. Maybe I'll see you later or something."

Steve strode away quickly while I stood there for another half-minute, realizing that before this morning, Vietnam had been abstract, something I read about in *Newsweek* and watched on television. Now it was real. Vic's life was over. I jumped when the bell jarred me out of my reverie. I shuffled off to class, recalling all the years I'd known him.

Vic—Victor John Cartier—had lived with his mom and sister, Renee, three houses down Summit Avenue from Steve. Vic was one of the two dozen or so kids who gave substance to the baby boom in our neighborhood in Webster Groves, a leafy middle-class St. Louis suburb. Over the decade-plus of our early and middle childhoods from the mid-1950s to the late 1960s, in larger groups we played endless hours of baseball, football, and kickball. In smaller sets of two or four, we roamed in and out of each other's homes, playing games, watching TV, and eating lunch and dinner with each other's families. Because of the age difference, Vic wasn't a significant part of Steve's and my life until we reached middle school. By then, Vic was going to the all-boys Christian Brothers College Prep school—a powerhouse in St. Louis high school sports—where they wore military uniforms, marched and drilled. Vic always had really cool cars: first a Pontiac GTO and then an MGB convertible. We hung out and watched as he and his best friend, Bob, worked on their cars. We ran errands for them and sometimes got to go for rides, speeding through Webster's sleepy streets and listening to Vic and Bob talk about their adventures that always involved some mix of football, girls, alcohol, drag racing, and cops.

By the time I was in high school myself, I had pretty much lost interest in hanging out with Vic and Bob, and even Steve. When I saw Vic, we would stop and talk, but we had less and less in common and little to talk about. Still, I wasn't totally surprised when he joined the Marine Corps right out of high school in late 1967. Over the next several months, while Vic was in basic training and then advanced infantry training, I had been reading everything war-related in *Newsweek* and the *St. Louis Post-Dispatch* and listening to Walter Cronkite give voice to his own disillusionment on the evening news. Antiwar protests were growing, and my parents, sisters, and friends had all been reinforcing my growing belief that the war was wrong.

By the time Vic came home on leave in early 1968 and was walking around the neighborhood in his uniform, the Tet Offensive was underway, and I was feeling more and more disillusioned about the war. It just seemed wrong, to me, that so many lives were being lost and a country was being bombed to pieces. I had no idea what to say to him when he told me he was going to be going to be shipped out to Vietnam after his leave. I didn't want to get into an argument about it, but I thought that if I were in his shoes, I'd be trying to get to Korea or Germany – anywhere but Vietnam. On the other hand, Vic was doubt-free about it. In fact, he said, this was what he had trained for, and he was looking forward to fighting.

As a 16-year-old living in Webster Groves, I found it exciting to learn about something important, happening in real-time and affecting our country and the world—and it was safely half the world away. But when Vic stepped on that mine on April 8, 1969, Vietnam became real. And very personal.

I realized at that moment that, in a little more than a year, I would have to make my first choice about Vietnam: What to do about the draft. Would I actually register? Or would I take the dangerous step of resisting?

The growing antiwar movement had within it a faction that advocated for active non-cooperation with the draft by not registering, or, if you were already registered, burning or turning in your draft card. I had read a number of firsthand accounts by self-described war resisters, and I was drawn to their clear sense of responsibility, conscience, and action.

Right then, it did not strike me as being terribly odd that, as a 16-year-old, I was contemplating some kind of action that could land me in court and in prison and, ultimately, shape the rest of my life. No more odd, I thought, than a decision Vic and many others had made to fight and that, ultimately led to their deaths.

* * *

My involvement in a youth-led movement that challenged my church's leadership the previous summer, in 1968, had made it possible for me to experience Vic's death as not just as a sad personal moment, but as a catalyst of my personal commitment to stop the war.

That year, I had turned 16, and I'd been confused by all I was living through. I was confronting my own wildly fluctuating moods and intense sexual attraction to girls and a few older women. I didn't know what to do or how to act. My internal turmoil was further compounded by the raging war in Vietnam, the assassinations of Martin Luther King and Bobby Kennedy, the riots in the cities, and growing protests on college campuses. I didn't know how to make sense of it all, especially in terms of the Christian faith I held so dear and had been the principal means I used to make sense of the world.

With all those thoughts and feelings swelling inside me, Sunday mornings, in particular, became an agony for me that summer. Everything was so family-oriented and it all moved in slow motion. After getting up early and putting on dress clothes, the four of us—-my sister and two brothers—Susie, David, and Steve—ranging in age from 18 to 10, were crammed into the back seat of our white Ford Galaxy 500 and driven slowly, methodically, by my father, the three miles over to Concordia Lutheran Church in the neighboring suburb of Maplewood.

After either Bible study or Sunday School, we had to meet up and sit together for the hour-plus church service. If my father wasn't sitting with us, it was because he was singing in the choir. He kept an eye on all of us from the choir loft and, on the drive home, would share his critical comments regarding our behavior. Once we were home, the second act of the Sunday drama opened, involving one of us boys riding along with Daddy to get Grandma from her downtown St. Louis apartment some 30 minutes away.

On one particular Sunday, I rushed upstairs to my room, hoping against hope that David or Steve would get the call. Instead, after about 10 minutes I heard:

"Paul! PAUL!! PAUL-O!"

"What? What? WHAT!?"

"You know what. Let's go, get a move on."

"Take David."

"David doesn't need driving practice. You obviously do, Mr. Yellow Light! Now! Let's go!" His sarcastic name-calling was a reference to my running a yellow traffic light when I had taken (and failed) my driver's test earlier that summer.

I slouched down the stairs, moved past my father and out the front door to the car, and got in the driver's seat. He came out five minutes later, saw me and started motioning with his hand to move over to the passenger side.

"No way am I driving with you on the highway, going downtown. Get over there!"

"But you said…"

"No. You watch me and learn. I don't want to risk it with you right now."

"But how can I—oh, just forget it!"

I scooted across the seat, buckled myself in, and stared out the side window. My father mumbled something, turned on the ignition, and backed out of the driveway. After five long minutes of driving in silence, Daddy turned the radio on. Loud.

* * *

Most Sundays, Susie was as happy as I was to have an excuse to get out of the house after our midday Sunday dinner. We jumped in the '54 Chevy sedan that she drove most of the time. She switched on KXOK and then turned it up when the commercial ended and the Beatles' *Day in the Life* came on. The Chevy had a manual shift on the steering column and I watched her working her way through the gears as we wound our way over to my friend Darrell's, a couple of miles away.

"How the heck do you do that shifting with all the other parts of driving? I don't think I'll ever get that. Well, if I even get my license."

She smiled. "Don't worry, you'll get there. If I can, you will."

We picked up Darrell and then drove the mile to Freedom School at Concordia Seminary. Susie dropped us off in front of the library, and we made our way inside toward a conference room on the second floor. As we walked up the stairs, Darrell pulled a brochure out of his back pocket, unfolded it, and passed it over to me. "Did you see this? Neeb had them on his desk. It's for the Walther League's convention up in Purdue, Indiana in August. Looks kinda interesting to me."

I slowed down and looked it over. "No, I didn't, let me see. Purdue … wow, it says they expect about 3,000 kids. That's big!" I passed the brochure back and asked, "You going?"

"I'm gonna try. Otherwise, this is going to be one long summer. It's right before my birthday in August, so maybe I can sell it as a birthday present or something."

We made our way down the hall and entered the small conference room. We nodded at the other kids in the room, pulled chairs out, and sat down next to each other. Chris, a pale, pudgy guy with a red, scraggly beard, was at the other end of the room, half-turned around in his chair and smiling and talking with Becky, his wife, leaning against the wall. She nodded her head toward us and Chris raised his hand in a half wave as they finished the conversation. My eyes followed Becky as she walked halfway around the room, pulled out a chair and sat down next to a girl sitting by herself. Becky was a sharp contrast to Chris. She was tall with long, dark brown hair and a tan; her sculpted legs and arms were evidence of her dedication to jogging and other sports. Having a chance to admire Becky up close for a couple of hours each Sunday was the original reason Darrell and I had been interested in the Freedom School program. Now that we had been attending for a few weeks, we had both discovered additional reasons to keep coming back. But Becky being there was still a major motivator.

Chris had just finished his first year at Concordia Seminary, the graduate theology school for the Lutheran Church-Missouri Synod, and was assigned to our church to gain some practical experience in pastoring at the parish level as he entered his second year of studies. He and Becky had been involved in the civil rights movement a few years before as undergraduate students. Following Martin Luther King's assassination in April 1968, they had come up with the idea of a racism education program for white suburban kids and named it "Freedom School" in homage to the "Freedom Summer" voter education and registration activities they had participated in in Mississippi. Chris and Becky had publicized their program to Lutheran teens in the suburbs largely by word of mouth. We were now beginning our third of the planned six Sunday afternoon sessions. A group of 10 of us, plus Becky and Chris, had gathered for each of the prior sessions. Today there were just six including Darrell and me, but the decrease in attendance did not seem to faze Becky and Chris, and Chris got the session underway.

I had always been a big reader, so the basic idea of the Freedom School—-reading a book each week and discussing it—-was a natural for me. What was new were the authors and the subjects. We had started with the *Narrative of the Life of Frederick Douglass*. Even though Webster Groves had a Frederick Douglass elementary school, the most I knew before I read the book that summer was that it was named for a famous slave and that it was the school where all the black kids in my town went before we got mixed together in Plymouth Junior High and Webster High School. The book and our group discussion had me thinking for the first time about the experience of slavery as lived by actual people: being bought and sold, being whipped, having no say in what you did every day, running away, and being hunted. The previous week, we had dived deeper into slavery and its Civil War aftermath by reading *The Souls of Black Folks* by W.E.B. DuBois. While much of DuBois' writing was hard for me to follow and completely understand, I came away with a sense of how much of our country's history had been hidden from my view and was totally outside of my experience—and that of my family.

But the book for this particular week—-*The Fire Next Time* by James Baldwin—-moved me in ways that I had never been moved before. First, it was contemporary. I had seen Baldwin on TV at some point—-probably on the news, probably after Dr. King was murdered. But by reading his book I came to understand—in a way I had not yet—how TV filtered ideas and turned them into bits of information that were shaped to make a point or fit into a theme of some sort. *The Fire Next Time* was full-on James Baldwin: heated, passionate, elegant, and brimming with pain. He drew me into his world. I walked with him in his neighborhood and felt I had been in his family's cramped Harlem apartment. I wanted to go back in time to his Pentecostal church and hear him preach as a teenager.

And I was so confused. Nothing in my life to that point prepared me to read James Baldwin. I knew I was part of the white America that enraged Baldwin, while having no idea how I, as a 16-year-old, could possibly have had anything to do with it. I thought I understood, but I knew I had no idea what this really was about, given my mostly white world. My parents were clear with us that racial equality was good and racism was bad. They argued with the neighbors about it and spoke up at church—-and encouraged me to go to Freedom School! But as I read Baldwin, I figured he would lump them in with the white liberals he disparaged. Baldwin's outrage and urgency, his demand for action, touched my own sense of impatience with my parents and their friends at our church: They were all talk and, in my eyes, then did nothing. Baldwin told me that if I was going to be real, I had to *act*.

That afternoon Chris and Becky listened to us. They asked a lot of questions. They had us read sections of the book out loud. While the six of us were all over the place in our reactions to the book, everyone had clearly read the book and jumped into the discussion. The hours flew by, and before I knew it, Chris was passing out copies of next week's book: *Nigger* by Dick Gregory. Before we left, Becky drew our attention to the last few lines of Baldwin's book and said she wanted to end the afternoon on a hopeful note. She thought we were going to be among "…the relatively conscious whites and relatively conscious blacks…" who, together, "…could end the racial nightmare in our country…"

We left the air-conditioned library by the same route we had come in and walked out into the blast furnace of late June heat and humidity. I inwardly groaned as I looked to the parking lot and saw Daddy waiting for us. We got into the car and he turned the radio off.

"Learn much in Freedom School? How was it?"

"OK, I guess." I glanced at Darrell in the back seat.

"Yeah, pretty good," Darrell added. Silence filled the car.

"Huh. OK then." My father turned the radio back to the ballgame, and we drove off.

* * *

The St. Louis summer sweltered along through the remainder of June, all of July and half of August while I spent most days working as a stock boy at Geggus' Market or hanging out at home reading or watching TV. Susie and I had become Eugene McCarthy supporters earlier in the year, and now, following the Republican convention that had nominated Richard Nixon, we spent hours reading and talking about the upcoming Democratic convention and what we were hearing about the antiwar protests being planned for Chicago. We had never attended a march, but we speculated together for the better part of an afternoon about how we could go to Chicago and join the protests. Our lack of connections with anyone involved in the antiwar movement, combined with the practical concerns we both had in managing our jobs and knowing that school would start just a few days after the convention was over, combined to assure that our plans never materialized.

In the meantime, Darrell had, indeed, talked his parents into letting him attend the national Lutheran youth group's—it was called Walther League after one of the church's founders, C.F.W. Walther—convention in Purdue, Indiana, scheduled to begin August 19, the week before the Democratic Convention. Since our church's Walther League chapter had been defunct for years, he was not going to be attending as a delegate, but Pastor Neeb had written a letter that secured some kind of status for him that allowed him to attend all the official business meetings along with the social and educational activities. His enthusiasm for the convention and the League grew with every mailing of background materials that he received in advance.

"Look at this stuff; it's really interesting," he greeted me when I walked into his room one evening a couple of days before he left. "Right here: They are going to change the charter and bylaws and everything and WE are going to be in charge of the League, locally and nationally. The National Council is made up of high school and college kids, and adults are advisors. Locally, they recommend the same thing. And it is all to focus on issues that we care about. Look at this stuff on hunger; it's something else."

I looked over the draft bylaws quickly, but spent more time reading over the colorful brochure on hunger, with maps and photos illustrating the problem across the world, including in the United States. One of the illustrations was labeled the "hunger chain" and named "racism," "war," "poverty," and other social problems as links in a chain that resulted in hunger. The call to action was pretty straightforward, quoting Jesus' command to "Feed the hungry." To a couple of nerdy high school almost-juniors who had "graduated" from Freedom School a few weeks before and still went to Sunday School, this was exciting, even intoxicating!

After a half hour of listening to him anticipate the wonders he was going to experience in Purdue, my enthusiasm for his projected adventures began to wane. I started yawning and acting bored, but in the back of my mind I realized how disappointed I was that I wasn't going with him. I wished him luck, walked out to my car, and drove off. I spent the next hour circling through the familiar streets of Webster Groves, car windows down, and blasting KXOK's top 40s rock from the Chevy's cheap speakers.

* * *

We pulled up to Rhonda's house about 3 on a Saturday afternoon in early October.

"Are you sure she's going to be here? I thought she was a cheerleader or something, and you guys had a game today?"

"Just shut up and get out of the car, Kuehnert," Darrell said. "It's just like all the other ones we've done. She'll either be here or not. And it is my high school and, believe me, I *know* who all the varsity cheerleaders are and Rhonda's not one. She says she hates sports."

We got out of the car and started walking to her house, a modest brick bungalow in the Dog Town section of the city. Rhonda was one of four kids and her family enjoyed celebrity status at our church because of her father, Earl. Mr. Weaver had just become the manager of the Baltimore Orioles in July and, in the last half of the year, had led the Orioles on a surge that landed them in second place in the American League. Even though Darrell and I were the farthest things from jocks, we were big Cardinals fans and knew baseball pretty well. Earl Weaver was known for his fiery temper, and I didn't know if I was more intimidated by the prospects of having to talk to the beautiful Rhonda or encounter the short, fiery Earl, who might not be pleased by two teen boys stopping by to chat with his daughter.

Fortunately, Rhonda's sister, Kim, answered the door and let us into the hallway while she went upstairs to find Rhonda. From the back of the house, we could hear the ball game—-the Cardinals were in the World Series with the Detroit Tigers. Mr. Weaver's shouted expletives punctuated the drone of the radio sports announcers. Rhonda bounced down the stairs, greeting us with a surprised smile and leading us into the living room, where she plopped into a wingback chair while we found seats across from her on the couch.

Darrell started his pitch. By now, we had done about a dozen of these new Walther League-related visits to the kids who were in our confirmation class at Concordia three years before and so, I knew exactly what he was going to say and where I was expected to pitch in a line or two. Darrell had come back completely fired-up about the organization and his experiences at Purdue. His enthusiasm was contagious—-first, completely infecting me and then, together, we had convinced Pastor Neeb to support us in creating a local Walther League chapter. It was the pastor's idea that we should go out and talk to all our classmates and invite them to a founding meeting. We naively didn't realize at the time that our agreeing to do so was a big win-win for him: He could test our sincerity and dedication, while at the same time, his boss, Pastor Meyer, and the church council would credit him with creating a new chapter.

Like every other kid we had talked to, Rhonda listened politely. She smiled a lot. Or maybe it just seemed that way as I tried to absorb the way the afternoon sunlight highlighted her red hair, the sprinkling of freckles across the bridge of her nose, and the way her legs looked folded underneath her in the chair as she listened to Darrell. My role was to be the closer, so I pulled myself out of my reverie and asked if we could count on her to attend our founding meeting that would be a week from Sunday, right after church. And like every other kid we had talked to, Rhonda said yes.

"Jesus, you were a little ga-ga there, don't you think?" Darrell punched me in the shoulder as we headed down the Weavers' front walk and back to the car. "Almost drooling, like you had never seen Rhonda before."

"I haven't seen her for, like, years," I said. "She was dreamy when she was 13 and in confirmation, I remember that all right. But, Christ, she has gotten incredible."

We got in Darrell's car and he signaled and zoomed down McCausland to our next, and final, stop.

"Well, you need to get a little more subtle there, Paulie. She enjoyed toying with you, I could see that."

* * *

As planned, the founding meeting of the Walther League Society of Concordia Lutheran Church, Maplewood, Missouri took place the second Sunday in October. Much to the delight of Pastor Neeb, nearly every chair in our Sunday school classroom was taken. Pretty much every kid we had talked to over the previous month from our class showed up, as well as a sprinkling of older and younger kids who had heard about it through the church bulletin or by word of mouth. We were flabbergasted by the response—and not at all prepared to run a large, formal meeting. Without a formal agenda, we made one up on the fly with Pastor Neeb's help while the rest of the kids talked and drank cups of lemonade that he had thoughtfully set up in advance.

Darrell started things off by thanking everyone for coming. He then gave a more detailed version of the Purdue gathering in August. He emphasized that more than 2,600 kids had attended as delegates from hundreds of chapters across the United States, Canada, and a sprinkling of other countries. Since Darrell had begun playing the electric guitar earlier in the year, he was particularly impressed with the music at the gathering and talked for a while about that. Folk music was the predominant form, as illustrated by there being more than 20 coffee houses with live musicians going every evening; one evening featured a jazz concert, and the worship services each day were major musical productions. He talked about some of the people and conversations that really impressed him: a farm kid from Crystal, Minnesota who was so passionate about hunger in the United States that he had drawn up a letter to President Johnson. He had spoken about it so effectively that more than 2,000 convention delegates personally signed his letter before he mailed it. A Black college student, Sterling Belcher, had moved Darrell and hundreds of other kids in a workshop session with his passionate, personal stories of racism's impact on his life and his community.

I then talked about what we hoped to do at Concordia. We had been in touch with the youth staffer for our region, Frieda Hamilton, and had learned that a handful of chapters were being formed in the St. Louis area. She was coming to St. Louis in a couple of months and would meet with us if we wanted. She also wanted us to connect with others who were planning a "Hike for the Hungry," a new idea that the Walther League had learned about from some Canadians that involved the participants getting donations in the form of pledges of dollars or cents per mile from supporters, and then "hiking" over a planned route in the community that was usually 12 to 18 miles long. The hikes served to both raise awareness of, and funds for, hunger. We also wanted ideas from all of them regarding activities we could do at our church to raise awareness of hunger and the related issues that the League talked about as the "hunger chain."

After leading a short discussion, Pastor Neeb got the group to vote to officially establish the chapter and to name Darrell and me as co-chairmen, since, he said, we were very motivated and had demonstrated our organizing skills. I could feel my face flush with embarrassment at Pastor Neeb's praise. I quickly scanned the room and saw all the smiling faces—surprised that nobody laughed at us or objected to the idea of Darrell and me leading the group. Pastor Neeb asked for a show of hands and everyone's shot up in favor of the motion. He asked everyone to donate one dollar on their way out of the meeting in order to pay our dues of 25 dollars to register as a Walther League Society. After a closing prayer, the meeting was over.

Darrell drove me home. We babbled a few minutes about the meeting and then fell silent. Neither of us reached for the radio knob, satisfied just to ride along with the sound of the wind coming through the open car windows. We were both elated and drained. We had no energy to talk about what we were going to do next. Before I got out of the car, I turned to Darrell and put out my hand. We looked at each other, grinned and shook. I didn't quite know what to do with the surge of emotions: pride, accomplishment, affection. I opened the door and quickly got out of the car, mumbling "Catch you later." I knew we had both prayed for this, but saying that out loud—let alone offering up some kind of prayer of thanks together—was not something we would do. I walked toward my front door while realizing that we had pulled off something nobody—not even us— really thought we could sunk in. I did think, "thank you, God," as I wondered if the warm feeling of accomplishment, coupled with a real feel of connection to others, was what Chris and Becky and even Pastor Neeb experienced in working for the church.

* * *

Darrell and I continued our Walther League efforts over the next six months, including making connections with other chapters in the area and with Frieda Hamilton. Naturally, both my parents and Pastor Neeb were enthusiastic about my attending a regional Walther League retreat planned for April in Houston.

While the program was all positive from my parents' perspective, and the registration fee was nominal, it was a stretch for them to pay for the transportation. To save money, they decided to send me by bus to Houston, and then fly me back, so I would not miss school. This irritated me no end. "Why," I had said, "can't you just be like everyone else's parents and buy a round-trip plane ticket? Why do you have to be so cheap?" I was sure that everyone else would know how I traveled and that I would be a laughingstock. I argued so fiercely that Daddy threatened to ground me for all of spring break and concluded by saying: "Just forget this whole thing—-YOU WON'T GO!" I stomped off to my room in tears. Mom later walked Daddy back from the brink. She came to my room and talked to me quietly and firmly: If I wanted to go, I would go on the bus. There was nothing else to be said.

But once I was on the bus that Tuesday evening, I began to realize that a 22-hour bus ride all by myself was not such a bad deal. For the vast majority of the journey south, the bus was half- to two-thirds full, so I was able to sit by myself. I filled the hours reading, writing in my journal, watching the scenery roll by, and listening to the conversations of my fellow passengers with particularly loud voices. I still remember the rhythm and cadence of the voice of the Black woman that got on the bus in Poplar Bluff, Missouri and "witnessed" about Jesus with the bus driver for the next four hours as he drove us into the Ozark Mountains, following the highway to Pine Bluff, Arkansas. Her voice followed me as I drifted in and out of sleep and disjointed dreams that night, first lulled to sleep by the rumbling motion of the bus, then startling awake as you do when you sleep sitting up and your head nods too far to one side or the other.

The sun rose as we entered Hot Springs and took a breakfast break for 45 minutes. I called my parents, ate some greasy eggs, and poked around the station's magazine stand, silently daring myself to buy a *Playboy* magazine. I took the dare and then hustled back on the bus, spending the next couple of hours hunched over my forbidden treasure. The remainder of the day unfolded languidly as, from Little Rock on through Texarkana and into eastern Texas, the bus traveled the secondary highways, picking up and discharging travelers in a parade of small towns and rural bus stops. I enjoyed meeting a few fellow travelers and having brief conversations, including a teen preacher who sat down next to me in his finely pressed black suit just a few shades darker than his skin. With his starched white shirt and deep red tie in sharp contrast to my jeans and T-shirt, he inquired politely as to whether or not I was saved. I said that I thought I was. That did not deter him from giving me the benefit of his standard fire-and-brimstone sermon, delivered in a soft voice with a Texas twang. We agreed that Jesus was our Savior, and shook hands as he got off the bus at the next town.

Getting back on the bus after a bathroom break in a small town in a stretch of rural Texas, I became aware that I was one of the few whites on the bus. Further, my clothes and books and suitcase marked me as being from somewhere else, in terms of both place—I was probably the only "thru traveler" from St. Louis at that point—but also class. I sat down thinking I was a long, long way from Webster Groves. My parents' economic circumstances had dictated that I travel by bus to Houston. Neither they nor I had any idea that the journey would be such a fitting prelude to the "live-in" I was about to experience.

* * *

Frieda and her husband, Mike, met me as I got off the bus in Houston. They had just picked up another early arriver, Jane Baue, from the airport. The four of us made our way out of the bus station to the parking lot and Mike's old Ford. Along the way, I stole a few sideways glances at Jane and thought that this retreat was already looking positive. I was even more encouraged when I found out on the car ride to Frieda and Mike's apartment that Jane was from St. Charles, Missouri—not exactly a St. Louis suburb, but only about 30 miles away. I took a shower at the apartment, ate with everyone, and helped load the car with sleeping bags, pillows, and suitcases. Mike drove us over to the Park Place Lutheran Church on the University of Houston campus. The large church basement, kitchen, and classrooms would serve as our home base of Walther League's Southwest Regional Easter Retreat over the next four days. Jane and I were joined by another 23 teens, plus a group of about four other young adults who, along with Mike and Frieda, were serving as staff and chaperones for the course of the weekend. A few other adults, including Pastor Alan Dieter, pastor of Park Place Lutheran and the head of the Lutheran Campus Ministry, would be with us off and on throughout the weekend.

Kids had arrived over the course of the day—primarily from Houston, Oklahoma City, Tulsa and St. Louis—and settled into the church's basement suite of rooms. One classroom was designated as the sleeping space for the boys and another for the girls. The largest room, adjacent to the kitchen, was a common space where we would have our meals and some group activities. Some of our worship services would take place in the basement common space, while for others, we would join members of the larger community in the chapel upstairs.

Frieda welcomed us and gave us an overview of the retreat schedule. We also learned we would be working together to make all of our meals and clean up. The adults had prepared our first meal since we had just arrived, but from then on, everyone would have to pitch in. Sign-up sheets for cooking and clean-up work circulated. Questions were asked and answered. Then Frieda turned it over to Pastor Dieter to kick off the live-in experience.

He asked us to stand up and move away from the tables into the large open space, and form into two circles, one inside the other. After we formed the circles, he told us we were now going to introduce ourselves to each other without words. Nervous laughter and chatter erupted: "What?" "How?" "You're kidding?" all could be heard above the grumble of the crowd. Pastor Dieter waited and we slowly quieted. "Look," he instructed. "You in the outside walk slowly in a clockwise direction; you on the inside, walk slowly in the opposite. As you pass each person, slow down and say 'hi' with your eyes. No talking now, go ahead …"

After a few seconds, the only sound was the shuffle of our feet as we walked slowly in our circles. After a few minutes, we were asked to stop and pair off with the person opposite of us at that moment. Each pair was to "go deeper" in their introductions, but still, non-verbally, although now we could touch if we wished. Again, nervous laughter as the pairs separated. After a few minutes, Pastor Dieter asked us to find another person we did not know and go through the same introduction. Then after a few more minutes, we switched again. The first two times I was paired up with two guys I had just met earlier, from St. Louis, John Bringewatt and Leroy Williams, both of whom attended Luther Memorial Church in Richmond Heights, the community just north of Maplewood.

My third pairing was with Jane, whom I had met at the bus station. As we looked into each other's eyes, I could feel myself beginning to flush, but I did not look away. When she lifted her hands up, bent at the elbows, with palms facing me, I mirrored her actions and then grasped both her hands. Our fingers entwined tightly, we kept our eyes locked. I smiled, and she reciprocated. Just then, Pastor Dieter called time and asked us to go back to the tables to discuss our experience together.

Over the course of the next 45 minutes, the Pastor skillfully drew everyone into a large-group discussion of our experiences in the nonverbal exercise. He talked about things like cultural norms and practices, terms I had heard but never given much thought to, let alone experienced through an exercise that challenged cultural practices around meeting strangers. While I was intrigued and fully engaged in the conversation, a corner of my mind kept pulling me back to the thrilling experience of looking deeply into Jane's eyes, holding her gaze and her hands. From time to time, I looked in her direction and once caught her looking at me. We smiled and both looked away, back to Pastor Dieter.

The opening session, pairing a new experience for us as a group with facilitated reflection by one of the retreat leaders, modeled how the next two days of the live-in would go. For most of our sessions, we were outside of the church basement, in various neighborhoods and agencies in Houston. The issues and learning sessions—around housing conditions, discrimination experienced by young people of color, the working conditions and treatment of farm workers, the global population explosion—were all expertly connected by Frieda with the core concept (develop the Walther League) of the "hunger chain." We also were brought into opportunities to act on what we were learning about: circulating petitions on a newly proposed Fair Housing statute for Houston; joining a multi-racial march honoring Dr. King on the first anniversary of his assassination; walking in a United Farm Workers informational picket line on the grape boycott outside a huge local supermarket; and organizing an Easter egg hunt for a group of little kids from a public housing project.

All of these activities and learning sessions were woven together into a coherent whole through informal time together spent in one-on-one or small group conversations throughout the day, as well as our work together in preparing and cleaning up after our meals and our worship services each evening. I can still remember the long, passionate talks I had over those three days with Frieda, as well as her friends and University of Houston students Jim and Corki, about all manner of issues related to Christian faith and, especially, the Vietnam War and the draft. Corki's husband, Jerry, was a conscientious objector who had elected to serve alternative service in the Houston Fire Department as a paramedic. He joined us for dinner one of the evenings and I had my first chance to meet someone who had successfully persuaded a very conservative draft board that he was indeed a pacifist while not being a member of a traditional "peace" church.

And then there was Jane. At the end of the first night's session, and again during each of the next two nights, we found each other and went off to a corner of the basement, sat on the floor, and talked. And talked. I didn't know how she did it then—although now I suspect it was a combination of her own ability to empathetically listen along with my strong desire to please her in order to have a sexual relationship—but Jane got me to open my heart like I had never done with anyone before. I shared what were then my deepest concerns and fears, ranging from my "stupid acne" and my "dumb crossed left eye," to the bewilderment, anger, and powerlessness

I experienced when faced with my father's depression. And as I listened to her, as well, and learned of her fears, hopes and dreams, we grew closer.

It was not a surprise to anyone, then, except perhaps me, that Jane and I were hanging all over each other during the Easter sunrise service and seemed to linger a bit too long when exchanging the kiss of peace after the Eucharist. We were both earnestly committed enough to the Walther League mission and building the movement that we spent time after the service with John, Leroy, Sherri, and Sue—the other St. Louis area attendees—to plan the expansion of the St. Louis Hunger Team that Darrell and I had started earlier in the year. We pledged to meet within two weeks of our return and exchanged addresses and phone numbers. The whole retreat group got back together for one more meal together before the Houstonians headed home and the rest of us headed to the airport. Jane's flight took off before mine that afternoon, so we had just a little more time to talk and make out at the airport before I watched her board and her plane take off.

My plane's departure was delayed for about two hours, so when I deplaned through the gate at Lambert Field on Easter Sunday night, Mom was standing there looking more tired than usual. She seemed to gain energy and become more alert, though, as I relayed the details of my bus trip and the retreat. I talked non-stop for the 45-minute ride home from the airport. Then, we sat up and continued talking for another hour at home. I conveyed all the details of the weekend except, of course, for anything related to Jane.

Talked out and exhausted as the clock in the dining room struck 12:30 a.m., Mom, mercifully, said that she would call the school in the morning and tell them I was sick. I kissed her goodnight and went to my room. I collapsed on the bed and looked around. Everything was the same and, yet, for an instant, the room seemed different somehow, maybe smaller. The trip to Houston had expanded my world in ways that could not be measured merely in the miles I had traveled. I had had conversations with kids and adults from a wide array of backgrounds and life experiences. We had seen poverty up close—-and listened to people who were actively working to end it. The worship experiences had made me feel fully alive and emotionally connected with others in ways that I had never known before. Really smart people I respected—Frieda, Mike, Jim, Corki, Pastor Dieter—had long conversations with me, answered my questions, and listened to me. And then, of course, there was Jane and our amazing kissing and holding and talking and kissing—all totally new to me. While the news of Vic's death had flipped an emotional switch in me the previous week, these retreat experiences made sure the switch connected me to a sense of purpose instead of despair.

I sat up and peeled off my T-shirt, stood and stepped out of my jeans, flicked off the ceiling lights, and lunged into bed. I wondered about Jane, half-forming a thought, and then fell sound asleep.

CHAPTER 2:
VIVA LA HUELGA!

"Viva la huelga!" cried Matt at the top of his lungs.

"VIVA!!!!" all 20 of us responded in unison at the top of ours. "BOYCOTT KROGERS—BOYCOTT GRAPES!!"

We repeated the chants over and over as we marched up and down the sidewalk alongside the Kroger grocery store in downtown Kirkwood, waving our picket signs emblazoned with the slogans we were chanting. The store was just a couple of miles from my parents' house, and I was pretty sure that one of our neighbors or church members would drive by and see me as they went about their Saturday shopping. The grape boycott was relatively new and still controversial, especially the grocery store picketing. The likelihood that some of my parents' friends would see me doing this and then, maybe, call them, made it doubly exciting for me that morning. I wanted to shake all of these suburbanites—especially my parents—out of what I saw as their complacency. If one of them picked up the phone and reported to my mom they'd seen me, I knew that would really get her attention.

Little did I know at that moment that the events that were about to unfold over the next few hours would not only get my parents' attention, but also that of the FBI.

After returning from the Easter retreat in Houston and learning of Vic's death in Vietnam, I was determined to get into the action. During the retreat, I had seen and heard firsthand how all the issues I was concerned about were connected to each other. Racism, poverty, the war in Vietnam, and world hunger were all tied together in a system that I now understood as fundamentally unjust and unfair, favoring the few at the expense of the many. Christians, especially, I thought, were required to respond to these urgent needs. To do otherwise was the height of hypocrisy in my book. And action required more than talking about things with your friends or just giving money to various causes. Action meant *doing*, real doing—literally putting your body on the line.

In Houston, our speaker from the United Farm Workers (UFW), Jorge, had told the story of his own work in the fields in California, Arizona and Texas. What he told us of his personal experiences of low wages, racial slurs, and terrible living conditions in the camps made me feel both enraged and somehow guilty—a confused set of feelings that I had experienced reading James Baldwin and talking about racism with Darrell. Yet I came away feeling connected with Jorge, and sure that the only way migrant farm workers could get better lives was by unionizing. Jorge emphasized that the best way for people who cared about farm workers to show their support was to join the national boycott of grapes that UFW was organizing to put pressure on the big growers. After his talk, I asked Jorge if the UFW had supporters in St. Louis. Before we left Houston, Jorge got a list of contact numbers to Frieda.

And so, the week after I got back from the retreat, I screwed up my courage and called the St. Louis contact number and connected with Matt, who was very welcoming. He told me that they met up with supporters every Saturday at 10 a.m. at the Teamsters' headquarters in St. Louis and went off in groups of 15 to 30, depending on the day, to as many grocery stores in the area that they could cover with picket lines for a couple of hours.

Now, in mid-June, after participating in the picket lines for almost two months, I was a veteran and had become pretty good friends with Matt and Verna, the full-time UFW organizers, as well as a handful of Teamster members and shop stewards who were regulars most Saturdays. My sister Susie had started to join me sometimes since she was home from college for the summer and was with me this particular Saturday morning. It was going to be my last picket line for a while, since I would be taking off in a week for a two-week long Youth Leadership Institute sponsored by Walther League in Chicago.

I was thrilled to have been invited to the Institute on Frieda's recommendation. I hoped I would be able to meet her and the national leadership's expectations of me. I was also secretly fearful that they would figure out I wasn't really cut out to be a leader and send me home. After the Institute, I would travel from Chicago to Denver, where the national convention of the Lutheran Church-Missouri Synod was scheduled to take place. The League was bringing as many of its youth leaders as possible to Denver to witness to the church's leaders about hunger and its root causes, as well as provide a "human face" for the League, as more conservative church leaders were beginning to attack it as it transformed to being "youth-led and issue-oriented."

So, a couple of days away from my seventeenth birthday—as well as the start of new adventures—I was in high spirits, marching and shouting outside the store. We had been there about 15 minutes when a KMOX-TV van rolled up and started filming us, with the reporter interviewing Matt on camera about the boycott. Just as Matt's interview was ending, Kirkwood police cruisers began arriving, pulling into the store parking lot, with lights and sirens going. The cameras kept rolling, but shifted focus to a police officer who got out of one of the cruisers with a megaphone and began addressing all of us in the picket line: "Attention! Attention! This is an illegal assembly! You are in violation of the law in the City of Kirkwood and must disband immediately. You have two minutes to disband."

I could feel my heart racing—this was totally outside my experience! I wanted to shrink away, but was carried along by the momentum of the picket line. As the cop was speaking, additional cars kept rolling up and about a dozen officers formed a loose line behind him in the parking lot. Radios crackled and the cars' bar lights kept flashing in the moments of silence that followed the announcement. Then, Matt and Verna swung into action, Matt walking over to the police with the cameras trailing behind him and Verna shouting encouragement to us on the line: "It's OK, it's OK. Keep walking, keep moving." Then shouting: "HUELGA! HUELGA! VIVA LA HUELGA!"

"VIVA!" all of the Teamsters responded while giving encouraging looks and nods to the rest of us, a motley mix of suburban housewives and high school and college students. " BOYCOTT GRAPES, BOYCOTT KROGER!!"

From 50 feet away, I watched as Matt seemed to become more agitated talking to the police officer, turned his back on him, and walked over to the picket line. This didn't seem like a good outcome to me. Matt got into the line next to one of the Teamster stewards, said a few words to him, and then joined in the shouting. The police officer stepped forward with his megaphone: "Time is up! Disperse now. Cease this illegal assembly immediately or you are under arrest."

Matt stopped walking and motioned and called us all over to him.

"Look. These suburban cops are dopes. We can walk on public sidewalks and exercise free speech. But, they won't listen and will arrest any of us that keep the action going. OK if you need to go, I understand, nobody signed up to get arrested. But, Verna and I and our Teamster brothers are staying put, and you can join us. We will likely go to jail though."

With that, Matt hoisted a *Boycott Grapes* sign and began walking down the sidewalk. Verna and the four Teamsters followed suit. I looked over to Susie and she said, "What the hell?" and joined the line again. I followed her, along with another three or four students whom I knew vaguely from previous Saturdays. The rest of our group faded off into the parking lot, while the cops watched those of us marching, our line of about a dozen now picking up energy and shouting again, while the TV cameras rolled.

"BOYCOTT KROGERS! BOYCOTT GRAPES! VIVA LA HUELGA!"

The leading cop had put his megaphone down on the hood of his car and now walked over toward the picket line, motioning the other officers to follow him. He stopped and stood in front of Matt. "You are under arrest for illegal assembly. Please come with me."

The officer took Matt by the upper arm with one hand while taking the picket sign out of his hands. Matt offered no resistance and looked toward the camera. "BOYCOTT GRAPES!" he shouted one more time as the cop led him over to his car, put the sign on the ground, opened the back door of the cruiser for Matt and guided him into the seat, closing the door behind him. He then watched as his men walked over to the rest of us to follow his orders.

The cop walking toward me seemed to be moving in slow motion. He had a slight grin as reached out and grabbed my upper arm while simultaneously grabbing a hold of one of my sister's arms. He turned us around and began walking us down the sidewalk toward his cruiser. I could feel my heart pounding, racing in rhythm with my thoughts: Was this really happening? Were they going to take me to the infamous juvenile detention center, where somebody was likely going to beat me up? Wouldn't Frieda and the other Walther League leaders be proud of me? Was I going to have a criminal record now? Forever? And what on earth would Daddy do?

Surprisingly, they put Susie and me in the same cruiser, and we had a minute to talk before the cops got in the front seat.

"Daddy is going to be livid! Why didn't you tell me this could happen?" she said.

"I would have left if you wanted to. Jeez!"

"Sure, sure. God, this will probably be on the news tonight and everything. Man, he is going to kill us for this," she said.

"Look, whatever happens, we're in it together," I reminded her.

"Right, sure, whatever. I hope we won't be in jail for a long time. Jesus, this is—"

We fell silent as the two cops got into the front seat, started the car, and gave a few whoops with their siren. I looked out the window and saw the TV cameraman still filming other arrests as we pulled away. The cops up front mumbled to each other and their radio crackled. They didn't say a word to us, and we kept our silence as they drove the five minutes over to Kirkwood's city hall and pulled around the back to park. They got out of the car, opened our doors, and each of them took one of us by the arm and led us into the building, up the stairs to the police department.

Soon there were 10 of us standing together in a group surrounded by a loose circle of six or seven cops in the reception area outside the police department in Kirkwood City Hall. Matt and Verna were smiling and joking with everyone. I realized that I had been trembling inside. I took a deep breath and looked over at my sister, who was talking to Verna like nothing special was happening. I found myself smiling a little, thinking that somehow, some way, this was going to be all right.

After a few minutes, the cop who had had the megaphone—and turned out to be the shift lieutenant—addressed us. He said we were going to be processed now and taken to cells. They had already contacted the municipal judge, who would be there in an hour or so to determine our bail and then, we would likely be able to get out of jail if we had someone to bail us out. He said this would apply to everyone who was an adult and that if anyone was under 17, they should let him know and they would call a juvenile officer and probably take them over to juvenile hall in Clayton. Susie glanced over at me and I shook my head, slightly, "no." I was three days away from my birthday, and there was no way I was going to get pulled out of this into the juvenile system. Neither of the other two students said a word.

We were told to line up in two lines, one of men and one of women. We stood in front of a desk sergeant who motioned impatiently for each of us to step forward, one at a time. As each of us stepped up in front of him, he glanced up, gave us a withering look, and barked out the same set of questions and commands:

"Name?"

"Spell it?

"Address?"

"Phone number?"

"Date of birth?"

"OK. Step over there for prints and pictures."

"Next."

When it was my turn, I subtracted a year and gave 1951 as my birth year.

"Almost your birthday, huh, fella?" the sergeant noted after I gave my information. "18 soon. This here is not going to be enough to get you out of the draft, though."

I smirked, moved over, and stood with the other men, waiting to get our mug shots and fingerprints done. I looked over to Susie in the women's line. For an instant, she met my eyes, smiled, rolled her eyes and shook her head as if to say she couldn't believe what I had done. Then she turned back and continued her conversation with Verna. When we had all been fully processed, a couple of cops shuffled each of the groups off to cells. We had two cells for the men in one section of the jail, while the three women were put together in one cell in another section. As far as I could tell, there were no other prisoners of either gender in the Kirkwood city jail that afternoon, but apparently they had protocols to follow that included segregating the sexes.

The expected one hour stretched into two, and then three. During the first half hour or so, we busied ourselves with chanting back and forth, between the men and women, repeating the slogans from the picket line. Soon, even we were bored silly by that. The Teamsters taught us some labor songs, like "Solidarity Forever," and everyone knew a few of the civil rights standards, like "We Shall Overcome." Soon enough, though, we had exhausted our repertoire and fell quiet. A few more minutes passed, and then I heard Susie's voice singing a round that she had learned years ago in Girl Scouts, "White Choral Bells." She and Judy and my mom knew a whole bunch of these rounds that my brothers and I thought were completely inane, but were always a part of long family car trips and singing around the campfire on our camping trips. "Jesus," I thought, "spare me from my sister's stupidity." She and Verna and the other woman in their cell kept at it for a while, though, and no one in our cells seemed to mind.

Matt and another guy stretched out on the steel shelf beds and fell asleep. The rest of us found seats on the floor. There was a little small talk and long stretches of silence. From my perch on the floor in the front corner of the cell, I could see down the hallway to the door that led back into the police station. I sat staring at the door, willing it to open, to no avail. I leaned my head against the bars, closed my eyes, and began to think about what would happen when we got home. Specifically, I wondered what Daddy's reaction would be and what might happen with him.

I wasn't worried that he would do much to us beyond, possibly, ground us for getting arrested—which struck me as absurd as I thought about it. But it was his go-to punishment for just about every infraction. He wouldn't react violently. He wasn't that kind of father, and likely wouldn't even raise his voice much; he rarely did. He loved to argue about what led to your misbehavior, as he saw it, and then pronounce grounding for days, a weekend or even weeks, depending on his own judgment of the infraction's severity. During the arguments, he would use sarcastic or cutting personal remarks ("no one with any sense would say such a thing") or religious pronouncements ("Jesus would weep to hear you say that") when he ran out of facts to bolster his point of view. He would never concede a point, let alone a complete argument. As a member of the family, you learned that once he got started, he would prevail and likely leave you exasperated to the point of tears.

But as I had gotten older, I was becoming aware that all was not exactly right with Daddy. Over the course of his adult life, I found out a few years later, he had been hospitalized a number of times with severe depression. In between hospitalizations were fairly long "normal" periods mixed with very depressed periods when he could barely maintain functioning at work and did little but sleep at home. When we were young children, during the times when Daddy was depressed and withdrawn, or seemed to be heading in that direction, my mother cautioned the five of us to be on our best behavior and not upset him. Whether she intended to or not, she conveyed to us that what we did could directly lead to Daddy becoming depressed and not being able to work, with dire consequences for all of us. So, that afternoon as I sat in the Kirkwood jail, I began worrying that our arrests might set off a chain reaction of sorts, resulting in Daddy being hospitalized again. He had, after all, barely avoided being hospitalized just six months prior, during the previous Christmas holidays.

I shut my eyes and slipped into my memories of that Christmas. Christmas was a big deal in our family. In addition to the home decorating, family gift buying, meal planning and relative visiting, there were multiple church services to prepare for and participate in. When my mom got the Advent calendar out of the closet and hung it up the first Sunday in December, I was already aware that this was going to be a different Christmas. First, not only was Judy out of the house for the second Christmas—as she had married the previous year; Susie was now gone to college at Southeast Missouri State and would just be getting home on the 20th. But, beyond this the strangeness of my sisters' absences, there was more: Something was going on with Daddy.

Each evening after work, he would walk in the house, take off his coat and—without saying a word to anyone—go into my parents' bedroom and lie down across the bed in the dark. Since their bedroom was off the dining room, I would sometimes stick my head through the door when I was setting the table for supper and tell him it was time to eat. Some nights he would get up and come in and join us, but not say anything, just eat and go back to his room. Other nights, he would just lie there and not say or do anything. From time to time, I could hear him sigh.

After dinner, David, Steve, and I would clean up. From the kitchen, we could hear Mom talking to Daddy. Sometimes you would hear something that you knew was his voice, but it was quiet and small, and the words unclear. Sometimes my mother could prevail on him to get up and go out to church for choir practice or a Wednesday service. Mostly, he lay there. She would become more frustrated and yell at him sometimes. We three boys in the kitchen just looked at each other and didn't say a word. We finished our chores as quickly as possible and got out of the house every night we could.

As the days counted down to Christmas, nothing seemed to be changing for the better. Mom had gotten Daddy to go back to his doctor, and he had started taking some medications. I knew from the last time I could remember this happening, about six years earlier, that he might just get worse: not go to work, start sleeping all day, and become totally non-responsive. That time, he had been on a work assignment in Denver for the summer. Our entire family relocated to a rental house in the Denver suburbs not far from where Daddy's brother and his family lived. We thought it was going to be a great summer vacation adventure together, and it had started out that way. Then he entered the downward spiral, as my mom described it, and withdrew. She eventually had to drive us all back home in early August, with Daddy lying curled up in the back of the station wagon. He was hospitalized for a few months after that and received electroshock therapy treatments, but eventually returned home and went back to work. Life went back to "normal" for us, marked by his strict rules about nearly everything, his sarcasm directed toward Mom, and his withering criticism directed toward all of us, most especially Judy and Susie.

My thoughts turned back to Christmas. Susie had come back on December 20 as planned, and that made the rest of us happy, but had no noticeable impact on Daddy. She helped Mom finish the shopping, baking, and decorating the house. My father had kept going to work and occasionally went to choir practice, but on Christmas Eve, a scheduled holiday for his workplace, he just stayed in bed all day. I went to work around noon at Geggus' Market. They were scheduled to close early, at 6 p.m., but Mom said I could miss the early service at 7 and just help Daddy get presents put around the tree and set everything up for the family Christmas Eve celebration that would start when she, Susie, David, and Steve got back from services about 8:30. Judy and her husband, David, would show up about that time, as well.

It was a very busy afternoon at the food market as neighborhood residents came in for last-minute groceries before the holiday. Ray, the assistant manager and butcher, set up the Christmas punch in the stockroom around 5. The other stock boy, Steven, clued me in to the fact the punch was spiked with alcohol, and he and I took turns going back to the stockroom and chugging punch, then returning to the front to bag groceries for customers and assist them to their cars. This was my first experience in drinking anything other than beer, and I was pretty buzzed by the time Mr. Geggus closed the door after the final customer and locked it, then took us all back to the stockroom for the party. The party simply involved a toast from Mr. Geggus, his passing out of pay envelopes with a Christmas bonus, and then another cup of punch before we all headed out.

The temperature had hovered in the upper 20s all day and was dropping now that the sun had set. There was a little dusting of snow on the grass surrounding the houses as I walked the three blocks home. I wondered if my speech was as slurred as Steven's had been by the time we left the store and was thankful for the cold air that seemed to be clearing the buzzy feeling out of my head a little. Our house looked cheerful with the holiday lights around the door, but I was alarmed when I looked through the windows and didn't see the Christmas tree lights or any other lights on in the house. I opened the door, walked into the living room, and turned on the desk lamp right inside the door. I took off my coat, gloves, and hat and threw them on the couch, then plugged in the tree.

"Dad? Daddy? DAD-DEE!!" I shouted as I walked through the living room, into the dining room, and pulled open the bedroom door.

"DADDY?!"

Not knowing what I was expecting, or fearing, I saw a shape under the covers, with a hand sticking out, holding the pillow over what must have been his head. Before I knew what I was doing, I had covered the distance to the bed and had pulled the pillow away from his hand and off his head. His arm and hand flopped back on the covers limply.

"DADDY? What the hell?"

I reached over and turned on the bedside table lamp. He turned his head toward me, his eyes flickering open for a second and then closing.

"Paul-o," he whispered faintly. His hand moved toward the pillow and he grabbed it and lifted it toward his head. I pushed his hand and pillow back down on the bed.

"No. NO. Come on. We've got things to do. Everybody is going to be back soon and YOU haven't done a THING! Get out of there, come on! It is CHRISTMAS, now get UP!"

His eyes fluttered open and shut again. He slowly turned his whole body away from me, a long sigh escaping from him. I sat on the edge of his bed and watched him. The sheet moved slightly, slowly with his breaths. I hung my head and rested my chin on my chest, feeling tears running down my face. I wondered what to do next.

After what seemed like an eternity, I eased off the bed, turned off the light, and walked out, closing the door behind me. I paused for a minute, then went down into the basement and pulled a large sheet off a pile of presents stacked on the big wooden table in the corner by Daddy's workbench. I stared at them, sat down on a stool, and rubbed my eyes with the heels of my hands. I sobbed a little, got up and went over to the sink next to the washing machine. I turned on the cold water and doused my face, again and again, until the sobbing stopped. I grabbed a towel and sat down again, staring at the presents.

After a while, I thought I heard some movement upstairs. Then I heard a toilet flush and the water rush through the drain pipe that ran along the wall above Daddy's workbench. Then some more movement and a couple of creaks from the floorboards.

I mumbled, "Shit, shit, shit," got up and grabbed as many of the presents as I could and took them upstairs, placing them around the foot of the tree. I repeated the process until all the presents were upstairs and arranged around the tree. I thought it looked pretty good. I went back down to the basement and sat down again, staring at the empty table. I knew everyone would be coming soon and didn't know what else to do. Then I heard some more movement from upstairs.

I turned off the basement lights and went upstairs to check out the sounds. As I came into the dining room, Daddy was coming out of his bedroom. He had not shaved for a few days, his face was puffy, and his scant hair mussed every which way. But he was dressed. He looked at me and immediately looked away. He grabbed a Christmas cookie off the platter on the table and walked into the living room without a word. I followed him. He sat down in the middle of the couch and looked at the tree.

"Milk?"

"Daddy, I…"

"Milk. And a plate."

I went into the kitchen and brought back what he had asked for. He took a bite out of the cookie and put it on the plate. He drank half the milk and set it on the table in front of the couch, next to the plate.

"Santa," he explained, and turned back to looking at the tree without another word.

The sudden noise of the outer door being slammed open against the wall jerked me back into the reality of sitting on the cell's floor on a June Saturday a little before 4. A couple police officers came through, clanged open our cells, and took us back into the reception area. An older man with glasses and a black robe was standing in front of the sergeant's desk. We stood in a semicircle around him, and he told us he was Kirkwood's municipal judge. He had set our bail at $25 each and said our court date would be in approximately two-and-a-half weeks. We were required to be there in person. We could now use the phone and make one call each to get our bail and/or get someone to pick us up.

Matt spoke up and thanked the judge. Then he told us he would call the union and they would have someone here as soon as possible to post our bond and give us a ride back to our cars. He walked over to the desk and made the phone call. In another 45 minutes, we were all bailed out and being driven back to our cars by volunteers mobilized by the Teamsters. Everyone was going to go out for food and drinks at a bar near Teamsters headquarters. Susie and I declined, thinking we had pushed our luck far enough.

We were right. When we got home, just after 5 p.m., Mom was just shy of pushing the panic button. When we pulled into the driveway, she was out the front door in a flash while Daddy came out of our detached garage in back, walking quickly toward us.

"Where on earth have you two been? You had us worried sick! You should have been back hours ago. Last week when you did this picketing you were back by 1:30. What happened? What took so long?" Mom's eyes were reddened and welling up with tears. Daddy's mouth was tightened into a small, straight line as he walked up to us, planted his feet, and folded his arms.

"Look what you've done: Your mother is a nervous wreck," he began, locking eyes with me. I felt my stomach tighten as I took half a step back from him and moved closer to Susie.

Susie began explaining in the low, sweet tones I had heard her use before when she was trying to get something, especially from our parents. I kept my mouth shut.

"Well, we were in Kirkwood all this time. The police in Kirkwood don't seem to like farm workers or the boycott or the constitution or something. Anyway, they arrested us all and—"

"ARRESTED! You two were ARRESTED! I can't—" and Daddy pushed in, talking over her. "They don't do these things just because! What did you do? What did you two do to get yourselves arrested in KIRKWOOD, for Pete's sake?"

Here we go, I thought, as I leaned in and shouted: "It wasn't just us two, Daddy, it was the whole picket line! Everybody that was there! The cops just came and said it was illegal and if we didn't stop, we would get arrested. So, they did—"

Just then, we heard the phone ringing inside. Mom hustled inside to get it. "Ted! It's for you!" Daddy turned toward the house and started to yell back, then thought better of it and quickly went inside and took the phone from her. We followed him inside and it became quickly apparent that it was Matt. Daddy motioned for Mom to get on the other extension and she went upstairs to do so. Susie and I went into the kitchen, got some water, and sat down at the counter.

"Man, I am glad he called. Great timing!" I said.

"Yeah, hopefully they'll listen and stop getting all weird. It wasn't our fault those dumb cops decided to arrest everybody. Jesus."

I could feel my heart slow to normal speed as I sipped the cold water. We sat in silence as 15 minutes passed, trying to hear as much as we could of Daddy's end of the conversation, but couldn't hear that much since he was two rooms away. My mind wandered back to what I had been thinking about when I was in the cell: Was this going to somehow set off another period of depression in Daddy? I didn't understand how, or if, certain things triggered it, but it seemed to me it was tied into stress or worry or something, either related to work or at home. While my parents never pretended that Daddy did not have depression, at that time in our life as a family, we never were engaged in any family therapy or even informally discussed questions or worries that we as children had. Each of us would find our way to some kind of counseling or therapy years later and have these discussions with our parents and each other eventually, but then, my 16-year-old worries and unanswered questions were a big portion of the emotional fuel driving many of the arguments with my parents—including the one that afternoon.

Finally, we could hear Daddy saying goodbye to Matt in a seemingly friendly tone. He hung up, and he and Mom came into the kitchen.

"OK, OK, it sounds like you two didn't do anything wrong. The Farm Worker guy—" he said.

"Matt," I offered.

"Right, Matt, says it was all on the Kirkwood cops. He had to convince me, but he said your group has done these picket lines all over St. Louis without a problem."

"I was trying to tell you that, Daddy, right when he called—" I interjected, and then stopped short when Susie gave me a sharp look.

"OK, but look, Matt works for the Farm Workers and you don't, so I think he knows a little more than you, Paul." Daddy paused. I grabbed my glass and drank the last of my water.

"Anyway, he says they have been having these problems in other cities, but this is the first time any St. Louis area cops have stopped a picket line. Maybe a test case or something. He is going to talk to his boss back in California about it on Monday. And he thinks the Teamsters here will pay have a lawyer for everyone at your trial. But then, I don't know about you two being represented by Teamsters, I don't think much of them."

"Oh, Ted, come on!" my mom interjected. "They're doing it for the Farm Workers. If they are willing to help out that's a good thing. You read that article in *Newsweek* about Cesar Chavez and you know how hard those poor people have it, picking those grapes and everything for pennies, really."

Susie glanced at me and raised her eyebrows. This was the first we were hearing that our parents had read anything about the Farm Workers. We thought they were pretty oblivious to why we were doing what we were doing on Saturdays.

"Well, I am going to talk to him more about it," Daddy said. "He said he would call me after he talks to his boss. We'll see about the Teamster lawyer after that. Anyway, he says you two did real good, that everybody behaved themselves, did the right thing, in the face of those Kirkwood cops."

"He thanked us and everything. And, and said ...you were brave," Mom teared up and pulled us out of our chairs into a hug.

Daddy looked like he might join us, then just patted us both on the back. "Anyway," he said, "we'll go to the trial with you in a couple of weeks. We'll just see what excuse the city of Kirkwood gives for stopping a peaceful picket line on a public sidewalk." He turned and walked toward the back door. "Now, let me go see why that lawn mower stopped working. Paul, I could use you to trim the grass along the driveway since you're done saving the world."

Susie and I looked at each other and smiled. Matt had saved our butts and, seemingly, won our parents over without much of a fight, with just 20 minutes on the phone. I wondered what exactly he said and how he said it. Later, Susie told me she had told Verna, when they were in the cell together, about our parents and how they were going to blow up. She said she figured that she and Matt were pretty smart about people and that's why they were good organizers. I remember thinking as I followed Daddy out the back door that, somehow, my sister had gotten pretty smart herself and even kind of fun to hang out with, and maybe I should spend more time with her.

As planned, I went to Chicago for the Walther League's Youth Leadership Institute the following week. The trial was scheduled for Tuesday evening, June 24, so Frieda arranged with my parents to fly me home from Chicago Tuesday morning, with the plan that I would return to Chicago and continue with the leadership program as soon as possible.

The trial took place in Kirkwood's Municipal Court, which was held in the city council chambers in City Hall. Typically, the court dealt with traffic violations and other misdemeanor offenses; it was generally a pretty quiet affair, involving a couple of dozen people and no press. We could see that this night was going to be totally different as soon as we pulled into the packed parking lot about 7 p.m. and saw TV vans there from all three channels. Matt and Verna had organized more than 70 grape boycott supporters, as well as Teamsters Union members, to show up to support the 10 of us who had been arrested. All these people were milling around in front of the City Hall entrance, where it appeared Matt was holding an impromptu news conference with a half dozen reporters.

Verna saw us and rushed over with a wide smile, crying "SUSIE!" at the top of her lungs, giving her a bear hug. Susie introduced her to our parents and then we greeted our fellow arrested picketers and joined the festive crowd as we waited for the doors to open and court to begin. Shortly, a couple police officers unlocked the doors, and we filed through the lobby, down a short hall, and through another set of doors into the council chambers.

We followed Matt and Verna to the front row and sat down with our fellow defendants. Soon we saw a middle-aged man with a wrinkled sports coat and a loosened tie rush in with his briefcase and make a beeline for Matt. This was our Teamsters lawyer, and Matt introduced him to each of us in turn. They then huddled for a minute before another man in a suit and tie entered from a side door and approached Matt and our lawyer. He was the City of Kirkwood's lawyer, and after a few moments of hushed conversation, the two lawyers walked off together and exited through the side door. Matt sat down with us and everyone chatted nervously.

I looked over my shoulder and scanned the room for Mom and Daddy, finding them sitting together in a row about three-quarters of the way back. Mom was talking animatedly with another woman sitting next to her. Daddy was looking around the room with a somber look on his face, seemingly taking in all the people. I tried to get his attention, but just then the side door opened, and the two lawyers walked in, followed by the court's bailiff, who announced "All rise! All rise! The Municipal Court of the City of Kirkwood in the State of Missouri is now in session, the Honorable Judge Harold Kiel, presiding."

We all stood as the judge entered the room and walked behind the City Council's desks that stood in a line at the front of the chamber. It was the same judge who had talked to us in the Kirkwood police station and set our bail that Saturday afternoon. He sat down at the desk in the middle, tapped the microphone there, and said: "Be seated." Then, as the room rustled into their seats he spoke again: "Counsel, please approach the bench."

Both lawyers moved forward from their tables and stood in front of the judge. The three men whispered together for less than a minute.

"Gentlemen, step back." The lawyers took a few steps away from the judge, but stayed at the front of the room.

"The defendants will please rise." We looked at each other and slowly got to our feet.

"Ladies and Gentlemen. We met on Saturday afternoon, June 14 here in the police station where you were charged with illegal assembly and parading without a permit and I set your bail. I am pleased to tell you that the City of Kirkwood has decided to drop all charges against all of you. Your bail will refunded. All cases dismissed!" He banged his gavel sharply and then added: "We are adjourned!" He stood up and marched out the side door, followed by the bailiff and the city attorney. The room erupted in cheers as all of us, now former defendants, embraced each other and shook hands with our attorney.

"VIVA LA HUELGA!" shouted Verna at the top of her lungs.

"VIVA!" we all thundered back. The call and response continued for the few minutes it took everyone to find their way out of the council chambers and onto the sidewalk. We walked out into the bright lights of the TV crews and their cameras. We shouted "BOYCOTT GRAPES" and "VIVA LA HUELGA" for a few minutes for the benefit of the cameras, and then quieted as the reporters gathered around Matt, Verna, and the Teamster lawyer to ask questions.

I had spied Mom and Daddy standing on the edge of the crowd during the spontaneous demonstration. Mom seemed to be totally into the spirit of the event, laughing and shouting along with the crowd. Daddy, not as somber as before but not smiling or shouting, looked pretty uncomfortable. Susie and I peeled away from the crowd around the TV reporters and found our way over to them now. Mom hugged and kissed us both, while Daddy smiled a little and started walking toward the car.

"Oh, I am so relieved, so relieved! This is so good that it's all over and the Farm Workers won! Ted, come on, don't you agree—it's so, so good!!"

"Sure, sure! It's good. This is how our justice system is supposed to work, though, so it shouldn't be such a big deal. And you kids are darn lucky. Lucky it turned out this way and you don't have anything permanent on your records!"

"Daaaddeee!" Susie rushed and caught up to him while Mom and I trailed a few steps back. "You can't say it was justice and it worked out the way it was supposed to and then say, in the same breath, that Paul and I are lucky! You can't have it both ways! We exercised our protest rights and—"

"No, you two are just lucky. Lucky you had the Teamsters and lucky Kirkwood didn't want to spend a bunch of money trying to make their point. Just lucky. This protest business is not something you want to do if you want to have a good career and you know that!"

"Oh, Daddy, jeez!" Susie protested. "Come on. We and the Farm Workers were in the right and we won, simple as that. Just like Martin Luther King and—"

"King is dead. Killed, all the good that protest did for him!"

"Ted! You are being ridiculous!" Mom walked up next to him on the other side from Susie and grabbed his hand. "Come on. We were worried and all that, but it worked out, everything's OK. Don't say these things."

We were now about 20 feet away from our parked car. Daddy shook off Mom's hand without speaking to her, picked up his pace, opened the car door, got in, and slammed it behind him. The car roared to life a moment later, and then sat idling with the solitary figure in the driver's seat staring straight ahead.

"I am just going to walk on over to Mel's house. He'll take me home later." Susie turned and started heading back the way we had come.

"Susie, no, come back here. Please," Mom pleaded. "You know he was just worried. Then he says hurtful things."

"No, no, I need to walk. I don't want to be around him anymore. Took a good moment for us and just turned it into crap. "

"Susan, you—oh, forget it! You call me when you get to Mel's and let me know you got there OK."

"Maybe."

Mom turned away from her and opened her own car door. I looked back and Susie was moving, heading back toward City Hall.

"Hey! Bye!" I shouted to her. She raised her hand in a wave, but didn't turn her head.

I grabbed the Ford's door handle, wrenched it open, got in the back seat, pulled the door shut. and sat back without a word. Daddy turned on his blinker and pulled out into traffic. I had no idea how to even start expressing what I was feeling. Susie was right—Daddy had taken a great moment for us and turned it to crap. I wanted to make him see that. I wanted him to say he was proud of us. I wanted to talk about how this experience was tied to what I had learned in Houston, what I was learning in Chicago, really, how the faith he and Mom had instilled in me as a child was now making sense. But I didn't have the words. Instead, the silence stretched tight between the three of us for the 15-minute drive home. It wasn't broken when we pulled into our driveway, parked, walked into the house, and went our separate ways.

I got up at six the next morning so that Daddy could take me out to Lambert Field for my 8:30 flight to Chicago. He wasn't much of a morning person and neither was I, so our silence from the night before stretched into the morning, but without the tension. As we got closer to the airport, he turned KMOX down to a whisper and asked me a few questions about what I was going to be doing in Chicago. He reminded me that his father had taken some graduate courses at University of Chicago, on another part of the campus but not too far from the Lutheran School of Theology where the Walther League Leadership Institute was being held. He parked the car in front of the terminal and walked in to the Ozark Airlines ticket counter with me. After I got my ticket, he looked at his watch, and said he really should be getting to work if I didn't mind him not seeing me off at the gate. We hugged, and I watched him walk out of the terminal before I turned and started toward the gate. On the way, I stopped at the magazine stand and bought a pack of Marlboro cigarettes. A lot of the other kids at the Institute smoked them, and I had tried them and liked them. I thought they helped me concentrate and, well, fit in with the others.

Forty-five minutes later, the half-empty plane was climbing into the morning sky heading north to Chicago. When the pilot announced that it was OK to smoke, I pulled the cellophane wrapper off the box, shook out a Marlboro, and lit up, fighting off a coughing spasm as I blew my smoke into the gray cloud that was forming quickly in the plane's cabin. I pushed my seat back and gazed out the window at the plane's wing pushing through the misty clouds. I smiled, thinking about the outcome of the trial the night before. I was already a bit of a celebrity at the Institute, being the only kid there who had been arrested in a protest of any kind. Now, this was going to be a great story to tell: How we were completely vindicated, all charges dropped, and all kinds of TV coverage for the boycott.

So much had happened in the 10 months since Darrell had gone to the Purdue convention and we had begun organizing the Walther League chapter at Concordia. Barely three months had passed since I learned of Vic's death and resolved to, somehow, make a real difference and stop the war. I was thrilled to be learning so much and taking action, putting what I believed were Christ's teachings to work in the real world, attacking the problems that caused people to suffer. Now, with my arrest, afternoon in jail, and our court victory, it seemed, I was really getting in the thick of things. Still, I felt that I was going to have to do more. The war was grinding on, killing hundreds of Americans and Vietnamese each week with no end in sight. And I was now a little less than a year away from my 18th birthday, when I would have to make a personal decision about the draft. No two ways about it, I thought, I was going to get even more "in the thick of it" if I was going to be true to myself and my faith.

Just a few years later, I found out that, if measured by drawing the official attention of the FBI, I was already in the thick of things. When I obtained portions of my FBI file in 1978, I was surprised to see that the first report in my file was of my arrest in the Kirkwood grape boycott picket line. As a totally new and naïve activist, I had no idea then that surveillance of Cesar Chavez and his supporters was a priority of the FBI—part of an extensive domestic spying program that actively involved local police departments like Kirkwood, and monitoring all types of legal organizing and protest activities. As I would soon learn, being spied upon by multiple police agencies for protesting was to be expected. Likewise, for those of us in more visible leadership positions of some type, being reported to the FBI was almost a rite of passage. Ironically, given the intent of the FBI to slow or stop these movements, these active surveillance efforts had a radicalizing impact on many of us.

But that morning, I was blissfully unaware that I was now a part of a growing database of identified "subversives." I took a couple more puffs on my cigarette, then stubbed it out in the ashtray in the armrest. I wrestled a while with my thoughts about Vietnam and what I was going to do about the draft, but nothing became clear. Instead, as the plane's engine droned, my eyelids flickered, and my thoughts fluttered. The next thing I knew a stewardess was shaking my shoulder, asking me to move my seat back up because we were landing in Chicago.

CHAPTER 3:
THE MOVEMENT: 1969-70

"**B**odie! BOdie! BODIE!" Susie called for me, using my childhood nickname. "Bodie, Bodie, come on!" she continued, coming down the stairs from the second floor to the living room. "BODIE where are you?"

I was ignoring her as best I could, since I had just that moment responded to our doorbell and found two men in suits standing on our front porch.

"Can I help you?" I asked them.

They flashed gold badges simultaneously and the older of the two spoke: "We're looking for Paul Kuehnert. We're from the Webster Police Department."

"Uhh, well ... that's me," I said through the screen, making no move to open the door. It was mid-October, but it was still warm and Daddy hadn't gotten around to putting the glass storm windows in the door. My heart began racing as I tried to remember what I could have done that resulted in these cops showing up at my door.

"Bodie, there you are!" Susie continued as she walked toward me. "Why on earth are you standing there with the door—" She stopped as soon as she saw the two men.

"Well, can we come in? We need to talk with you," said the taller of the two cops.

I pushed the door open with my trembling hand and said, "Well, I guess, I mean …" my voice trailed off and they stepped into the living room and saw Susie.

"And who might you be?" asked the same cop who had spoken to me.

"His sister." Susie folded her arms across her chest and stood next to me a few feet inside the front door.

"Name?"

"Susan. Who are you, exactly? I didn't hear before."

"Detectives Scavata and Hendriks from the Webster Police. We just need to talk to your brother."

"About what exactly?"

"Do you go to Webster High, too? It's about school. But it was only Paul that was mentioned."

Hendriks had a notepad out and was scribbling away—when he wasn't staring intensely at me. My heart felt like it was going to explode, and I was sure that everyone there could hear it booming.

"No, I don't, but I think I will stay," Susie said. "Our parents are at work and I think they will want to know what is going on." I couldn't believe how calm and collected she was. I shoved my hands in my jean pockets to wipe the sweat off my palms.

"Suit yourself," Hendriks said. "Now, Paul, we understand you were one of the students involved in the moratorium activities Wednesday at the high school, right?"

"Well, there were hundreds of us—"

"Yeah, yeah," Hendriks interrupted, "but didn't you organize one of the whatever-you-called-it, seminars or—"

"Teach-in. We call it a teach-in."

"OK, teach-in. And who was doing the teaching, then? Regular teachers? Students?

"A bunch of different people. Students. Teachers. Speakers from—"

"Outside speakers?"

"Sure, different people."

"Paul, didn't you bring a guy named Dennis Cummins in to speak at this so-called teach-in?"

"Sure, Dennis was there," I said.

"And what was his purpose?"

"The same as everyone. Talking about the war and the draft and stuff."

"Stuff. Stuff like what?"

"Just what I said. How we can all work together and stop the war."

"Didn't he talk about SDS? Wasn't he there to get you kids to form an SDS chapter at Webster High?" he pressed.

"SDS is one of the groups working against the war, so I guess that might have come up. It was really all about the war."

Susie had been hanging back a little as I was being questioned, but took a step toward Detective Scavata. "You seem to know all about it. Were you there, too?"

"No. People complained and they told us—" Scavata said.

"People?" Susie and I said at the same time. *Man*, I thought to myself, *I am glad Susie is here.*

"Yeah, students, parents, teachers. People. Look, Paul, we wanted to tell you that Dennis Cummins is a big agitator. Nobody wants a radical, outside group like SDS here in Webster, at our high school. There is no need for outsiders at the high school. We want you to know that for the future, OK?"

I didn't know what to say as I felt myself shift from being afraid to being angry. What the heck were these guys doing here? I had just read an article in *Liberation* magazine, the monthly publication of the War Resisters League—which I had joined at the end of the summer—about the FBI and police in some big cities hassling civil rights workers and antiwar activists, but Webster police? Our sleepy little suburb? I shook my head slightly, remembering that the article concluded by advising anyone getting such a visit should say nothing to the police or FBI—or at least as little as possible.

Before Susie said anything else, I spoke up: "OK, OK. Well, thanks for stopping by," and pushed the door open. My move seemed to stop the detectives short.

"Yes, well, remember," said Scavata, "This Cummins guy is not welcome around here, especially at Webster High. Let your friends know that, too." Scavata and Hendriks filed out the door, and I closed it tightly behind them and watched out the window as they climbed into their unmarked brown Ford sedan and drove off.

"Jesus, Paul, what is with you, anyway?" Susie asked. "I'm glad I got to witness Webster's finest protecting us from … what again, exactly?"

"Ourselves? My friends? Man, I can't believe this actually happened!"

"And Cummins, Cummins. Don't I know that name somehow?"

"Sure. You met my friend, Kathy. The dangerous 'outside agitator' is Denny, her brother. He is a draft resister, of course, but they didn't even seem to know that. Christ, almighty." I moved toward the stairs to use the phone and call Kathy or Joe or Anne, the other kids from our high school group involved in the Vietnam Moratorium. I stopped and turned back toward Susie. "Oh, and what did you want anyway, shouting my name all over when those cops came up," I asked. "No wonder I couldn't think straight."

"I have no idea. Maybe it will come back to me later, Mr. Agitator."

* * *

I had met Denny Cummins more than a year before, when he was canvassing our neighborhood for the Democratic candidate for U.S. Senate, Tom Eagleton. Denny was a slightly built, buttoned-up college student at that time, politely talking to my parents on our front porch about Eagleton's opposition to the war. I had come outside to listen. Denny was very friendly and introduced himself to me, asking if I knew his sister, Kathy. I mumbled something along the lines of "not really," and he encouraged me to look her up.

I didn't know it at the time, but Denny had already decided to return his draft card to the Webster draft board, along with a letter protesting the war. By the time Detectives Scavata and Hendriks came to my house, Denny was the public face of the draft resistance movement in St. Louis. After he returned his draft card in late 1968, the Webster draft board had reclassified Denny as 1-A and, shortly afterward, issued an induction notice. He refused induction later that year and was tried and convicted in a St. Louis federal court. When I met him, Denny's case was on appeal and, while he awaited the outcome, he was working full-time for the American Friends Service Committee training volunteer draft counselors and staffing a number of other antiwar activities. I reconnected with Denny when I went through the draft counseling training course at the St. Louis Peace Information Center. We really hit it off and stayed in touch afterward, talking occasionally after Peace Center meetings about what it meant to be a draft resister. He was easy to talk to and encouraged me to think deeply about the impacts—both positive and negative—of not registering for the draft.

Now, months later, Kathy and I had become good friends through our antiwar activities at high school. I sprinted up the stairs and dialed Kathy's number. She answered and I excitedly told her about the two cops interrogating me. She wanted to hear more details and agreed to swing by and pick me up so that we could talk further as we headed over to the St. Louis Free High School (FHS) potluck dinner. The FHS was a very loose collection of 50 or 60 high school kids from Webster, Maplewood, University City and two or three private schools in the area that had been organized at the beginning of the school year. FHS met most Friday evenings at Eden Seminary, hosted by a couple of seminary students.

The core of the FHS had formed around Mary Beth Tinker, a senior at University City who had become famous for recently winning the free speech case *Tinker vs. Des Moines Board of Education,* which ruled that the wearing of black armbands to protest the war was a right for high school students. The FHS shared information about antiwar protests and provided a level of coordination to the moratorium protests. Members also organized their own classes on a wide variety of topics, ranging from poetry to math and history.

Kathy swung into our driveway in her green and white Volkswagen van and beeped her horn a few times. I shouted goodbyes to Susie and my brothers, slammed my way out of the front door, and jogged over to the van. Ann Grace was sitting in the other front seat so I slid open the van's side door and clambered into the back seat. Ann and Kathy both turned around in their seats, grinning at me.

"SOoooo!" they said simultaneously. I paused and took in the crazy contrast of my two friends for a second. They couldn't be more different in their appearances: Kathy—in her bobbed, brown hair, light make-up and fashionable clothes—would be seen most in our high school as a "socie" (short for "society girl"), meaning a conformist who embraced the middle-class values and lifestyle of white teenage suburbia. Ann—with her homemade cape, torn jeans and careless tangle of blond hair—was pure hippie. The three of us had connected with each other in the classes we shared and built our friendship at the beginning of the year based on our common interests and experiences in one or more of the overlapping social circles we were a part of: "politicals" (kids who were active around the war, racism and the draft), "artists" (kids involved in writing for or producing *Potpourri,* the official high school creative arts magazine), and "freaks" (kids who actively flouted middle-class dress and personal appearance standards and cared mostly about getting high).

I grinned back at them and relayed the tale of Scavata's and Hendriks' visit pretty much as it had unfolded. After listening for a minute, Kathy jerked the gear shift and backed out of the drive in a hurry. It took us just over five minutes to cover the short distance from my house to Eden Seminary where potluck was about to begin. I was finishing my summary of the Webster cops' interview as we got out of the van, walked over to the seminary library, and found our way to the large basement conference room.

As we entered the room a few minutes before the potluck was set to begin, I was taken aback by the large number of kids in the room—easily 70 or so, whereas usual attendance was no more than 20. Ann had brought a large plate of brownies she had made that afternoon and Kathy had two jugs of lemonade; I blamed the Webster cop for distracting me from my plan to grab something from the fridge at the last minute. Ann and Kathy took their contributions over to the table while I talked with Diane, one of the Eden seminary student hosts, and took in the crowd. I nodded to a few friends from Webster while making my way over to Darrell and his friends from Maplewood, Joe Warnhoff and Bob Moss. Together they had launched their own "underground" student newspaper, *Free Fall*, at Maplewood that fall.

"Hey, man! Hot off the presses!" Darrell called out as he handed me the new issue of *Free Fall*. It was mimeographed, four double-sided legal pages stapled together. "You're on page 2!" I glanced at the first page—all about the moratorium and the war—and flipped it open to see my article about Matt and Verna and the grape boycott. They had also published one of my short poems that I had shared with Darrell on a whim.

"Thanks, man, it looks good! How many of these did you guys get out?" I asked as I pulled out a chair and sat down across from Joe.

"Just about 200 or so on Wednesday morning as folks were going into the building—" Joe started.

Bob chimed in: "Would have done more, but they called the cops on us and we had to stop when we saw them coming. We learned from last time and stashed all the extras in my car trunk as soon as we saw the cops.

We just went into school with the crowd from the buses and they never even saw us."

Before I could find out more, we were interrupted by Diane who had climbed up on a chair and emitted a couple of piercing whistles. The room fell into stunned silence.

"Sorry to interrupt, guys," she said, "but we want to get started with the food and the program tonight! Welcome to St. Louis' Free High School! This is the only high school that is run completely by students!"

Cheers and whistles interrupted her for a few seconds. She continued: "Since this is a seminary, we have a few traditions, a few requirements when we break bread together here. We give thanks or say grace. So, let me say a nondenominational blessing and then let's grab some food and sit down and we'll rap. Here goes!" Diane folded her hands in front of herself, squeezed her eyes shut and shouted: "Good bread, good meat, good God, let's eat!" and jumped off the chair to laughter and clapping.

We made our way over to the food, filled our plates and sat back down again. Kathy and Ann joined us. It turned out that Kathy knew Joe from the previous summer, when they had both worked as day camp counselors at the South Side YMCA. Ann introduced herself and began reading *Free Fall*. As I ate, I looked around the room and let the energy of the animated conversations and laughter wash over me. I felt happy and grateful, coming from a sense of having found people I belonged to and with. I only knew a few of them very well, but that night, sharing a meal in a library conference room, I felt a true, very tangible spirit of connection to this loose collection of earnest teenagers who cared about the same things I did and were acting on their convictions. It was the same feeling that I had experienced during my afternoon in the Kirkwood jail and throughout the Walther League Leadership Institute in Chicago, and even at Frieda's retreat in Houston the previous spring.

I had two languages to describe these experiences and feelings: political and religious. The political language I used to describe my feeling was being a part of "the Movement," the amalgam of antiwar and civil rights activists who were seeking fundamental change in our country—a movement you joined by showing up and being active. The religious language I used described being a part of a much longer, even more fundamental community, the disciples of Jesus Christ. Because of my Walther League experiences, the two were becoming blended. I had begun to believe I could not be a true Christian without acting on my beliefs in the world in ways that took on the modern manifestations of sin and evil—namely, war and racism.

After about 15 minutes, Diane again interrupted the buzz of conversations and gave a report about the moratorium's activities and impact. She talked about the estimates of more than 2 million involved in demonstrations and teach-ins across the country. She included an overview of the actions that had taken place on every college campus in St. Louis and nearby, including the University of Missouri in Columbia and the University of Illinois campuses in Edwardsville and Carbondale, all within a couple hours' drive of St. Louis. We then listened to reports from the high school leaders in the room. Kathy gave the report from Webster and concluded with a reference to my being visited by Webster police detectives that very afternoon. Diane then handed the meeting over to a special guest, Yvonne Logan, from the St. Louis Peace Information Center, to discuss plans for the moratorium in November, focused on a national demonstration in Washington, D.C. We all eagerly took Yvonne's flyers about how to get a space on the buses that would be going to D.C. from St. Louis.

After the meeting broke up, Ann and I rode around Webster with Kathy in her van for an hour or so, talking animatedly about the November demonstration. As we circled through the downtown area of Webster, I stared up at the offices of the Webster draft board, a second floor suite of offices above some of the small shops at the corner of Lockwood and Gore. I wondered if we could stop the war or at least get Nixon to declare some kind of ceasefire before I turned 18, now only eight months away. I remember that I felt pretty hopeful that night, thinking if there was a ceasefire I could justify obeying the law, apply to be a conscientious objector, and not have to face the terrible choice of resisting the draft.

* * *

And while I loved spending time with my more political friends like Kathy, Joe, Darrell and Ann, a big part of me was drawn to the creative, counter-culture world of kids that were mainly into music and dope. Some of these friends, like Peggy O'Connor, would turn up at our protests and even some of the Free School classes and potlucks. It was unclear if Peggy had been kicked out of Nerinx Hall, the all-girls Catholic high school a few blocks away from Webster Groves' public high school, or if she had convinced her parents that they were wasting their money. As I got to know her, she told me stories of numerous suspensions from Nerinx—for smoking and for skipping class—while keeping an air of mystery around how exactly she came to Webster as a senior.

By the time of the October moratorium, Peggy and I were spending more and more time together after school. The routine became that we would hang out with Ann and others of our mixed group of politicals and freaks for 20 or 30 minutes, smoking and talking, and then peel ourselves off, getting on my motorcycle and speeding the half-mile to her house. I would park the bike in her driveway, and we would go upstairs to her family's apartment in the two-family frame house that sat on the corner of Cedar and Gray. Her mom and little brother would be in the kitchen, where we spent some obligatory minutes answering questions about the day, drinking water or milk and scarfing down some kind of snack. We would then go off to Peggy's room to "study," which mainly involved sitting or lying on her bed, talking and listening to music. Our musical tastes were pretty compatible, although I tended to like more folk and she liked more rock. Bob Dylan worked for both of us, so we listened to his albums more often than not.

That fall, Dylan had released "Nashville Skyline," which was much more acoustic and uncomplicated compared to "Blonde on Blonde" or

"John Wesley Harding." One afternoon, we were listening and singing along with "Lay Lady Lay," when Peggy made a half-roll from where she was slouching on pillows on her bed over to me and began kissing me. Before this, I had never really thought about Peggy as a potential girlfriend. She was my friend and I liked talking with her and smoking the occasional joint. But, being unattached to anyone else and enjoying her soft lips and darting tongue, I happily kissed back. As we embraced and I rubbed her upper arms and then up and down her back through her blouse, I noticed something was missing: There were no bra straps across her shoulders or back. Having never before faced such an opportunity, I started to rub the side of her chest under her arm and began rolling Peggy from on top of me to over on her side, and then her back. After I managed one full-handed grasp of her breast through the fabric of her blouse, she pushed my hand away, broke our kiss, and whispered, "No, not here, not here—" and sat up.

We were both flushed and breathing rapidly.

"Peggy, I, well, I—"

"Shush. It's all good; we just need to get out of here. Let's go outside, maybe go over to the park."

She stood up, brushed her long, brown hair back from her face, and fussed with her skirt and her blouse a little. She jerked the turntable's arm and needle up, cutting Dylan off mid-croon. I stood up and she grabbed my hand and pulled me out of the bedroom, then led me into the kitchen, where she dropped my hand quickly as her mom looked over at us from the stove.

"It's too nice of a day to be in here doing homework! We are getting out and taking a walk around before Paul has to go home for supper."

"OK," her mom said, "but we are going to be eating soon too, so don't be gone too long. Bye, Paul."

"Bye, Mrs. O'Connor. I, um, well, thanks."

Peggy grabbed my arm and yanked me into the stairwell, and we both started laughing as we rushed down the stairs. Once outside, we ducked down the driveway into the back yard, and I pushed her up against the back wall of the house and began kissing her again. Peggy quickly broke off our kiss and turned her head to look across the street to the park. The park was a tiny affair, kitty-corner from her house, occupying the corner of that block with a depth of 150 feet or so in each direction, before running into the fences of the houses that ran alongside it. Somehow, it had been spared being acquired by one or another developer in the past century and so was occupied by a stand of tall oaks and maples that were currently decked out in an array of orange, red, and yellow leaves. At some point, the city had added a curved, brick-paved path that bisected the park, as well as a variety of bushes that provided a lush understory for the miniature forest. Other than an aging park bench and an ancient drinking fountain that no longer worked, the park was unoccupied.

"C'mon, let's get over there, before my dumb brother comes out here."

We cut through the back yard, glanced up and down the street, and crossed. Without a backward glance, Peggy grabbed my hand and led me off the sidewalk and into the park. It was not overgrown, so was easy to walk around the forsythia bushes that lined the edge of the brick path-way. We made our way toward the back corner where the shadows were already deep and stopped in front of a clump of lilac bushes. We embraced and began kissing again, this time touching and rubbing each other's bod-ies without constraint. We found a way behind, and under, the cover of the bushes and were on the ground awkwardly tugging open each other's clothing. I awkwardly maneuvered myself in between her legs and low-ered myself toward, and then, in her. She pulled me down to her chest and thrust her pelvis up almost at the same instant. We bucked and kissed for what was both an infinity and an instant, and, finally, quieted, my head nes-tled between her shoulder and neck, my penis deep inside her warmth, still twitching from time to time. Minutes unwound. The occasional car passed.

"Umm, this is getting a little, uh, hard, or something," Peggy said.

"Oh, no, I'm sorry, I mean, I don't want you to feel bad, or—"

"No, no, just, like, get off, get up."

"Oh, oh, yeah, sure, sorry."

I pushed myself up to kneeling and began fumbling with my pants. Peggy sat up after pulling her skirt down. She reached over with both hands and pulled my face to hers, and kissed me.

"So what am I?" she asked.

"Uh, what do you mean, what are you?" I asked

"I mean, like, what number or whatever? How many girls have you balled?"

"Well, really, OK, well, really, you are my first, Peggy, and—"

"I have NEVER been anyone's FIRST! Jesus GOD!"

She began laughing as she buttoned up her blouse and then grabbed her panties and began wrestling them on from a sitting position. I could feel my face flush.

"No, no, Paul, it's OK, I'm just like, really happy, really happy for you and for this. It's so great—but look, we better get out of here and both of us need to get home, right?"

"I guess, yeah."

I led the way, duck-walking out from under the bushes and stood up. I turned around and helped Peggy stand, pulling her close to me as she did. We kissed again, deeply, and I held her tightly and began rubbing against her.

She broke our embrace and pushed me back, slightly.

"Come on. Help me get brushed off, and you, too," she said as she pulled some leaves out of my hair. "I don't want you getting grounded or something."

I brushed off the back of her blouse with my hand as she began moving toward to path. I caught her hand as she stopped short when we stepped onto the path and nearly ran into a young woman pushing a stroller. The woman startled—and then relaxed and began smiling, shaking her head slightly.

"Sorry, lady!" Giggling, we rushed down the path, to the sidewalk, and looked across to Peggy's house. Some lights were on in her house and her father's car was parked behind my bike that I had parked diagonally about two-thirds of the way down the drive.

"Oh, he is going to be pissed. Don't come in or anything, you better try to get going before he sees you and starts yelling about how he told you to park on the street."

We hurried across the street and into Peggy's yard. I gave her hand a squeeze and ran over to the Honda 90, slapped on my helmet, and kicked the bike to life.

"Oh, hey, bring my books to school for me, will you?" I asked.

She nodded. I pushed the motorcycle around the side of Mr. O'Connor's Chevy Impala, revved the gas and took off down the driveway and into the street without looking back. After a mile winding through the residential streets, I came to a busy intersection with a stop light and pulled up at the end of the line of cars. Waiting for the light to turn green, I absentmindedly adjusted my helmet's chinstrap and smelled Peggy's tangy scent. The light changed, I downshifted and pulled away behind the cars, wondering if my parents would notice that something major had changed about me when I sat down at the dinner table that evening.

* * *

The following Saturday evening, I picked Peggy up on my motorcycle and we rode over to the Loretto-Hilton Center for the Performing Arts at Webster College to hear Father Daniel Berrigan speak. A member of "the Catonsville Nine," Father Berrigan—along with his brother, Phillip (also a priest), and seven others—had been convicted of taking nearly 400 files of men classified 1-A from the draft board office in Catonsville, Maryland and setting them afire with homemade napalm in the parking lot. All of the files were reduced to ashes while the nine resisters stood together holding hands, praying and singing. They were appealing their conviction, and Berrigan was on a tour to promote his book, *The Trial of the Catonsville Nine,* and raise money for their legal defense.

Daniel Berrigan had become a hero of mine, because he was living and acting the way I had come to believe all Christians must in this time of national crisis. I was bubbling over with excitement that I would get to see and hear him in person. Plus, I was doubly thrilled to be sharing this experience with Peggy, whom I now considered to be my girlfriend since we had had sex earlier in the week. The fact that she and I had not actually talked about our relationship in the few days since our late afternoon tryst in the park was not something I had given much thought to. To the extent I had thought about our relationship, it was along the lines of figuring out how we could have sex again, not about my feelings for her, or her for me, or for our future.

Peggy and I were both wearing our standard hippie garb of jeans and flannel shirts, along with jean jackets, despite the fact that the temperature had fallen to about 40, so we were red-faced and quite chilled after the short ride and eager to get into the warmth of the theatre. As we entered, I saw a handful of acquaintances from the St. Louis Free High School, as well as Denny Cummins. Denny waved us over to the small group he was with in a corner of the lobby. I introduced Peggy to him and he introduced us to his wife, Jane, and a handful of other members of their community, McPherson House, a group of 15 or so activists who lived together on the west side of St. Louis; there, they baked and sold bread, ran the editorial operations of the *St. Louis Free Press*, and supported a variety of community organizing projects.

The lights flashed as a signal for us to move into the theatre and take our seats. Peggy and I tagged along with Denny, Jane, and the others and found seats as far forward as we could. The theatre held about 750 and was nearly full when the lights dimmed, the footlights came up, and Father Berrigan strode onto center stage to thunderous applause. With the practiced ease of a preacher, a poet, and a university professor, he held up his hands to silence the crowd and began by reciting part of his "Meditation on Catonsville":

"… All of us who act against the law turn to the poor of the world, to the Vietnamese, to the victims, to the soldiers who kill and die for the wrong reasons or for no reason at all, because they were so ordered—by the authorities of that public order which is in effect a massive, institutionalized disorder. We say: killing is disorder, life and gentleness and community and unselfishness is the only order we recognize. For the sake of that order, we risk our liberty, our good name.

The time is past when good men can remain silent, when obedience can segregate men from public risk, when the poor can die without defense … We have chosen to say, with the gift of our liberty, if necessary our lives: the violence stops here, the death stops here, the suppression of the truth stops here, this war stops here."[1]

For the next hour he spoke, telling a series of stories about his personal faith journey, reciting a number of his poems, as well as passages from the Gospels. He wove it all together into a powerful, coherent message: Our times demanded that we resist the war if we called ourselves Christians. I was spellbound, captivated by this short, slight, impish priest, his bright white collar set off by his simple black suit. Not only was I drawn to what he was saying, but *how* he said it: his lyrical delivery, his presence that filled the room and somehow made me feel deeply connected to him and to everyone in the darkened auditorium.

---

1. "A Meditation from Catonsville" by Daniel Berrigan, pp. 69-70, in Delivered Into the Resistance: Essays by the Catonsville Nine-Milwaukee Fourteen Defense Committee, Advocate Press, New Haven, CT, 1969.

When he finished, we all stood and the applause was deafening, lasting for a couple minutes. He stood on the stage smiling and then, as the lights came up, he made his way down off the stage and simply walked up the nearest aisle into the audience and began shaking hands and talking with people. Our seats were right on the aisle, so Peggy and I stood waiting as he slowly made his way up the aisle toward us. As he ended a conversation and a few people stepped away from him, Peggy stepped forward with her hand out toward Father Berrigan. He shook her hand and I came up and stood beside her. He looked from her to me, smiled, and then shook my hand as well. We had each mumbled something by way of a greeting and Father Berrigan looked back and forth at us again and said: "Ah, you two are lovely. So glad you could be here. I think there is a party afterwards somewhere here on campus. You should find out and come!" I was starstruck and couldn't think fast enough to choose one of the dozens of questions I wanted to ask him. Instead, Peggy said, "Thanks, Father! That would be fun. See you later, maybe."

He shifted his attention to a small group of men who had pushed up beside us. "Brother David!" he exclaimed as he embraced a studious-looking young man in horn-rimmed glasses, "I was hoping you would be here!" We turned away and made our way up the aisle, into the lobby and out of the building, back into the chilly night. I put my arm around Peggy and pulled her close to me as we walked over to the bike.

"Oh my God, he was so amazing, so good! If we had priests like him at Nerinx maybe I would have stayed!" she exclaimed.

"I think maybe I should become a Catholic," I said.

"Oh, that is crazy talk. Most of them, most of *us*, are not at all like him, let me tell you. Like the stupid priests at Holy Redeemer where my parents drag me—"

"Ok, maybe not just a Catholic, but I need to be a Jesuit!"

"JESUS!"

"Exactly!"

We had reached my motorcycle, and Peggy pulled me up to her and kissed me. As we kissed, she moved her hands down my back to my butt and then slid quickly to the front of my jeans and rubbed my penis. I was startled and jumped.

"Yeah, if you go Jesuit you can't do any of this, well, at least you're not supposed to."

"Hmmm, that is true. I guess I better stay Lutheran and we can keep this going and I can still be a resister like him. He is just amazing, I never heard someone put everything together like he did." I was holding Peggy as I said this, and I could feel her shift slightly. Then she stood back, dropping her hands from my waist.

"Hey, it's cold and you are way too serious," she said. "Get me home before we freeze."

I suddenly felt confused, unsure about what exactly was going on. I pulled Peggy into a hug and then looked into her eyes: "Peggy, you are beautiful, and I love you."

"You are one silly boy."

"No, you just said I was serious and I am. I really love you, I think."

"You think? No, Paul, you are really sweet. I think you are in love with the idea of me."

"I, well, no. I know. I love you, Peggy, the physical, real you, not the idea of you. What does that even mean?"

"Think about it some. It's mainly physical between us and, like, that is good, that is OK. You think because of balling me that you should love me. That's loving the idea of me. You don't know me, not really, not yet, maybe not ever, who knows?"

"I, but, well…" I sputtered into silence, feeling mixed-up and hurt. Peggy pulled the helmets off the handlebars and handed mine to me. It was like clamping my head into a bucket of ice as I strapped it on, got on the bike, and kicked it to life. Peggy climbed on behind me. We zoomed out of the parking lot and retraced our path through the dark streets to her house. She hopped off at the end of her driveway, gave me a quick kiss and handed her helmet to me, saying nothing but good night. I watched her walk up the driveway and wave to me as she went in her door. I revved the engine in response and turned down the deserted street toward home, overcome by a rush of feelings—frustration, sadness, anger, confusion—flooding over me in waves. I became aware that I was speeding, the bike seeming to be an extension of my feelings as I opened the Honda 90 up as far as it would go on a couple of stretches of Summit Avenue, hitting 80 and blowing through a series of stop signs. I was on our street in a flash and took the turn into our gravel driveway too fast, the bike skidding and almost dumping me. I killed the engine, got off and wheeled the bike into our garage. I took off my helmet and wiped my wet face with my jacket sleeve, convincing myself that the tears were just a product of the cold wind in my face, nothing more. I slammed the garage door shut and trudged into the house.

* * *

Everyone I knew wanted to go to the national moratorium march in Washington that November 15, but only Ann and I succeeded in getting permission to miss a day of school and cajoling our parents out of the $30 for the bus ride and another $40 for a hotel room for Friday night. So, after school late Thursday afternoon her mom gave us a ride to the St. Louis riverfront where the line of chartered Greyhound buses taking St. Louis marchers to D.C stretched on for blocks. We found our way to the bus that was filled with kids we knew from the Free High School and plopped into a couple of seats in the middle of the coach. The bus filled up quickly. I was excited to be going and to be able to spend the time with Ann. Of late, we had been spending more time together during the school day, with our group of close friends after school, on weekends, and for long periods on the phone. Over the course of the fall, I had been considering Ann as a good friend, but I was beginning to feel more for her, both romantically and physically. After my series of short-lived relationships—with Jane (ending a few weeks after I got back from the Walther League Leadership Institute), Mary (a member of my creative writing class that I fell head-over-heels for in early September; she had told me "it just isn't happening" a few weeks later), and most recently, Peggy—I was hoping that building romance on the foundation of what seemed like a strong friendship would lead to a more lasting relationship. I thought that the long bus ride might provide the perfect opportunity to see if Ann shared my interest in taking our relationship in this new direction.

As the buses finished loading, we watched out our window as hundreds of antiwar demonstrators who couldn't make the trip held an impromptu rally to send us off to D.C. in high spirits. Shortly after 5 p.m., the buses began to move out as everyone inside and outside the buses chanted "PEACE NOW!" As our bus made its way from the riverfront to the highway and across the Mississippi River on the Poplar Street bridge, the chanting was replaced by a sing-along ("If I Had a Hammer," "Give Peace a Chance," "Blowin' in the Wind") that finally faded into an excited buzz of conversation. Ann and I settled back in our seats and effortlessly picked up one of our numerous threads of ongoing conversation. We shared the snacks we had each brought along. I felt relaxed and happy as minutes, and then hours, rolled away along with the miles as we sped east. Eventually, the coach became quieter as conversations trailed off. Ann made a trip to the bathroom and punched off the reading lights over our seats when she returned, announcing that she wanted to sleep. She spread her blanket poncho over both of us, snuggled up to me and put her head on my shoulder. I took one of her hands in mine and sighed. In the very faint light, I could see that her eyes were closed, and I heard her breathing slow. I stretched my legs under the seat in front of us and closed my eyes thinking that maybe Ann would be my girlfriend like I had begun to hope.

I awoke with a kink in my neck and Ann's knees pushed into my right side. Sometime in the night, she had shifted positions, and her head was now resting between the window and the side of the seat. I could only imagine how her neck was going to feel when she woke up as I peeled myself out from under the poncho and made my way back to the bathroom. When I returned to the seats, Ann had shifted herself again and pulled the poncho totally over her head. I rummaged in my backpack for some fruit and the novel *Siddhartha* by Herman Hesse—our homework for my humanities class. I read, watched Ann sleep, and viewed the mountains of Pennsylvania as we worked our way toward Washington. Finally, Ann roused herself, and we fell back into our conversation. Neither one of us had been further east than Indiana, so we spent a lot of time watching the scenery, especially as we made our way into the D.C. metro area.

Shortly after noon, the bus pulled up to our hotel in northwest D.C. Famished, we dumped our things in our respective rooms, then found a diner in the neighborhood and ate our first meal in almost 24 hours. Over lunch, we discussed our plans for the demonstrations: that night's candlelight March Against Death for the more than 45,000 U.S. war dead and then the main march and rally on the Mall Saturday morning. Ann had not been planning to go to the March Against Death, while I had made plans to connect with Pat Krause, the associate director of the Walther League, her husband, Paul, and others from the church-based peace movement in Chicago to join the march that had been organized by the American Friends Service Committee. We agreed to go our separate ways for the rest of Friday and meet back at the diner at 8:30 Saturday morning before heading to the march and rally together.

I headed back to my hotel room to dig out Pat's letter for the address and phone number of her friends in the Georgetown neighborhood that she and Paul would be staying with. I found it and went to a pay phone in the lobby. Before calling Pat, I called my parents back in Webster to let them know I had made it to Washington. Since the call home was collect, it was very brief. Even so, I could hear the worry in my mother's voice as she asked a number of questions about the bus, the hotel, and my plans for the next 36 hours in the nation's capital. Even as I emphasized how safe everything seemed and that I would be spending most of my time with Pat and others from the church, I inwardly marveled at how much freedom my parents had been giving me over the past year. Looking back on it now, I think it reflected at least three interrelated factors. First, they trusted me and believed in my sincerity. I was earnest and grounded all that I did as an activist in the language of our Christian faith. Second, they increasingly shared my views on the war. They explicitly told me that they were willing to give me the $70 for this trip out of the belief that I was going on the march representing the whole family. Finally, despite the riots of the previous year following Dr. King's assassination, they viewed our country and its cities as safe places for a boy who was nearly 18. While this may have been somewhat naïve, they were not totally outside the norm amongst their peers. So, while they worried, I enjoyed my independence and gained great experiences.

After talking with Mom, I gave Pat a call. She told me how to get to her friends' apartment via the bus. I got a walking map of the area from the front desk, found the street that Pat told me the bus would be on and took off on my adventure. About an hour later, I was ringing the doorbell at the apartment. Pat introduced me to a roomful of people, most of whom were from Chicago and connected with faith-based organizations. Pat and I had a chance to catch up a little bit about Walther League business and before I knew it, it was time to head over to Arlington to join the march.

As Paul drove a group of us out to the assembly point near Arlington National Cemetery, Pat shared how the March Against Death was being organized. It had started the day before, on November 13, and each hour, 1,200 marchers left the assembly point to walk solemnly to the White House. Each marcher carried or wore a placard with the name of a U.S. service member who had been killed in Vietnam and, when reaching the White House, were to speak or shout out the person's name, take off the placard, and put it in a large coffin-shaped container. I was pleased to learn that if you knew someone who had died in Vietnam you could create a name placard for that person and carry it to the White House. Pat shared that the march organizers feared that they would never attract enough marchers to memorialize all of the dead, but that, so far, the response had far exceeded their hopes. They were more than halfway through the names, with about 12 more hours to go.

We jumped out of the Krauses' car near the assembly point, and Paul went off in search of a parking place. As we joined the back of the line that seemed to be a hundred or so deep leading up to the tables distributing the name placards and, since it was getting dark, candles poked through eight-ounce paper cups. I was struck by the hushed, almost solemn mood of the crowd that had gathered beyond the tables.

Most of the marchers took placards with names that had already been prepared, but when I got to the table, I asked if I could have Vic Cartier. I was directed over to another table with a stack of blank poster board and a bunch of black markers. I quickly made my own placard that read "PFC. Vic Cartier, USMC," punched holes and looped string through it, then paused, staring at Vic's name. Vic's face flashed in front of me for a second, and I wondered if he felt anything when he stepped on that mine. "Jesus, give us peace," I mumbled to myself, unsure if I was praying, and shook my head to clear it. I hung the placard over my chest and raced off to catch up with Pat, Paul, and the others. It was now dark and quite chilly as a steady breeze blew off the Potomac, just a few hundred feet away. Finally, just after 6 p.m., a man with a bullhorn told us to light our candles and walk in pairs. We were about halfway back in the crowd from the starting point, and it was quite moving to see the line of candlelit marchers begin to stretch up and over the bridge and into the National Mall on the other side of the river.

I fell into step alongside one of Pat's friends and we began walking quietly toward the bridge. Since this was my first time in Washington D.C., I felt completely awestruck when we reached the middle of the bridge and I could take in the full expanse of the Mall, with its monuments and reflecting pool stretching back to the brightly lit White House in the distance. As I walked and absorbed the scene—hundreds of shuffling marchers holding candles partially illuminating the names of the fallen entering the center of our national memory—my thoughts turned to Vic again, remembering our last conversations. I wondered if he had stayed as confident about the rightness of the war once he got to Vietnam. Thinking about his ready sense of humor, though, I knew that whether he had turned against the war or not, that marching against death in the war, and his death in particular, would be OK with him.

It took nearly an hour for us to cover the two miles separating Arlington from the White House. As we approached the mansion, the route of the march was illuminated by sets of portable searchlights set up behind the fence and pointed toward the marchers. Behind the lights, we could make out masses of what we assumed to be either police or troops guarding the President (news reports had made us aware that Nixon was inside the White House and would not be "distracted" by the likes of us protesters). As we approached the front entrance, our double-file line narrowed to single file. Each marcher paused at the front gate and we either quietly said—or loudly shouted, depending on individual preference—the dead service member's name. As I approached, I resolved to make sure Nixon heard Vic's name, and shouted "PRIVATE VICTOR CARTIER!" at the top of my lungs.

We then continued to march on down Pennsylvania Avenue to the U.S. Capitol. We slipped our name placards off as we approached a dozen black caskets set up to receive the names we had carried. One by one, we stepped forward and deposited our name placard in the casket. Each time a name was placed in a casket, a drum sounded. I was surprised to find that tears were welling up in my eyes as I made my way over to Pat and Paul. Pat hugged me and said, "Let's go find some food!"

* * *

Ann and I met the next morning as planned. Over a rushed breakfast in the crowded diner we had found the day before, we exchanged stories about our activities the previous night. Ann had hooked up with several kids we knew from Free High School and walked over to the Lincoln

Memorial. They discovered a few impromptu folk concerts happening around the reflecting pool, shared a few joints, watched the March Against Death from a distance, and made their way back to the hotel after they decided it was getting cold.

As we sat and talked in the diner, we had a view onto the street, and we both noticed that there seemed to be almost a constant flow of people streaming by in the direction of the Capitol. It was fairly early—about 8:30 on a Saturday morning—and that seemed a little strange. After paying our bill, we made our way outside and joined a constant stream of people walking up K Street toward 6th Street NW. As we turned left on 6th to head toward the Mall, we found ourselves part of a growing mass of people that, as we walked along, began spilling into the streets. We had originally planned to make our way over to Pennsylvania Avenue via E Street to join the march that was starting at 10 a.m., but by the time we got to E Street, we saw that we were moving into an even greater mass of people that stretched for blocks, both toward the Mall and toward Pennsylvania Avenue. We decided to forget about marching, given the size of the crowd, and try to get into the Mall and as close to the Washington Monument as we could so that we would be able to hear the speakers and the music.

By the time we got to the Mall, it was nearly 10 a.m., and we were unable to get much beyond the area just below the Smithsonian Museum of Natural History, around 10th Street. People were streaming into the Mall from every direction, and the area around the Washington Monument and north, toward the Ellipse, was a solid mass of people. Colorful banners and signs with a wide range of peace slogans were everywhere. We found a spot relatively close to some large sound system speakers in the hope that we would be able to hear the speeches when they got started. Soon we were surrounded by standing and sitting people and decided to plop down on the ground ourselves, sitting on Ann's blanket poncho and huddling together for warmth.

We soaked it all in: the people, the bright blue sky with wispy clouds scooting by, wafts of marijuana and cigarette smoke, occasional rousing chants of "Peace Now!" and related slogans. Soon music began, and we strained to see the stage, to no avail. Fortunately, the sound quality was decent. As noon approached, the crowd swelled with the tens of thousands of marchers who had walked the length of Pennsylvania Avenue from the Capitol. The rally got underway with speakers ranging from Dick Gregory to Senator Gene McCarthy, and musicians including Arlo Guthrie and Peter, Paul, and Mary. As speaker followed speaker, I began losing interest in what was being said. I was relieved when, by midafternoon, it was clear that the rally was winding down. The crowd began to thin and there was enough room to move toward the stage. We made our way forward and got within 150 feet or so of the stage.

We hung there a little while longer and, while I don't recall any of the speakers' words now, I do remember the strong feelings that washed over me as the rally ended: of pride, that we were such a huge, unified and peaceful crowd; of belonging, that I was connected to all of these kindred spirits working for peace and justice; and of hope, that surely, with such a massive display of opposition to the war, President Nixon would realize that making peace was the only realistic choice—and that the war would surely end very soon.

And although it has been documented that the October and November 1969 moratoria stayed the administration's hand and prevented a major escalation of the war that fall,[2] it took only a few months until Nixon would order the invasion of Cambodia and propel me beyond any remaining doubts I had about the need to resist the war and the draft with every fabric of my being.

---

2. See pp. 375-79, The War Within. America's Battle Over Vietnam by Tom Wells, University of California Press: 1994.

CHAPTER 4:
DECISION TIME

At first, I thought the incessant BRRRRRRRRRRING! was part of the dream I was having. Slowly it dawned on me that it was the phone ringing and, apparently, no one else was in the house or, if they were, they weren't answering the phone.

I threw the covers back and swung my legs over the side of the bed smack into the metal framing cot that Joe slept on when he stayed over. His parents had kicked him out of their house, and he was staying with various friends as he struggled to stay in school and reconcile with his parents. He was currently staying with Jeff Gillis in Ladue but planned to return to our house around New Year's Day since we were closer to Maplewood's high school.

"Fuckin' A!" I yelled at the top of my lungs and hobbled off down the hall to the phone outside my sisters' bedroom. I grabbed the receiver.

"Hello?"

"Hello, may I speak with Paul, please?" The man's voice sounded familiar, but I couldn't place it.

"Uh, sure, sure. This is he."

"Oh, great, so glad I reached you, Paul. This is Mr. Knight up at the High School and—" He paused as if something on his end of the phone had distracted him. My mind was racing, wondering why on earth the principal of my high school would be calling me over Christmas break. It had to be something I did, but there had been no demonstrations or teach-ins since the November moratorium. As far as I knew, I was passing all of my classes. I had even been dressing for gym and participating despite the harassment from the jocks in my class about my long hair and "girls in the locker room."

"Uh, sorry. Somebody here in the office knocked on my door. Anyway, I am glad I got you. Don't worry, it's nothing bad; in fact it's good news, I think. We have been reviewing senior records here, checking to make sure that everyone is going to be set for graduation. We have found a number of students that have already met all of their requirements for graduation, right now, at the end of this semester. And you, Paul, are one of them! I am calling to see if you want to graduate in January, instead of June. You wouldn't have to come back from winter break, even. You'd be done right now! What do you think?"

I was speechless. This was incredible! I hated that place and felt like I had so much to do for Walther League and the Free High School and the antiwar movement. What an amazing chance to start doing what I *wanted* to do instead of what they *made* me do every day.

"Paul, you still there?"

"Yes, yes sir. This is, like, hard to believe. Are you sure?"

"We have double-checked everything before making the call."

"Well, I guess, yeah, I mean, sure. But don't my parents have to OK this?"

"Yes, of course, but I wanted to see if you would be interested before writing them a letter with all the details. I'll do that now and put it in the mail. Hopefully they'll get it tomorrow and call me. We will need to all have a meeting as soon as we can. You can tell them about it, though, and they can call or just wait for the letter."

" OK, OK, I will. Thanks a lot!"

"OK, goodbye for now. I'll see you soon to get this done!" He hung up.

I put the phone in its cradle and turned toward the bathroom to brush my teeth, thinking all the while that there was something behind this sudden offer of early graduation.

A few days later, I was a free man. Everyone I knew and talked with about it—including my parents—believed the sudden offer of early graduation was directly related to my being seen as a protest leader. But since they all knew how much I hated school, they agreed I should see it as a gift and not worry about it as long as I got my diploma. So now, on what would have been the first day back in school following Christmas break, I was lying in bed smoking cigarettes, listening (at the highest possible volume) to Dylan's *Highway 61 Revisited* for the millionth time that morning and chatting with Joe about the lyrics in between songs. Joe was back staying with us and sleeping on the cot after his two weeks in Ladue. He had also decided to leave high school behind, but, in his case, without the benefit of getting a diploma.

Hours and at least a pack of cigarettes later, we had worked our way through every Dylan album a couple of times and were fully into Jefferson Airplane's *Crown of Creation* when my mom burst through the door, waving her hands exaggeratedly as if she had to clear her way through the smoky haze as she walked over to the record player and snatched the arm up, cutting Gracie Slick off mid-phrase.

"I guess you two have had quite the relaxing day, huh?" she asked as we sat up in our respective beds.

"After working all day, I guess it's my job to clean up after your breakfast and lunch and whatever else you've been doing with coffee and tea and whatever?"

"I, well, we—" I started.

"No, no, I'm not finished. Look, it's well and good that you are both done with high school. Fine. But don't think you are going to have this kind of life now! Oh, no! Each of you have two choices: Find a job or do all the housework here every day. Cleaning. Laundry. Dishes. Probably even cooking! But you two are not sitting up here all day, every day, smoking and sleeping and having a great time until you decide to go to some demonstration or something. This room stinks to high heavens, like locker room and bar combination with all this cigarette smoke." With that, she strode to the other side of the room and pulled the balcony door open, letting the cold January air rush in. "—You two get up now and strip these beds and let this room air out before your father gets home, Paul. Get the laundry going and then both of you get in the kitchen and help me clean up and get dinner going. It will be your first lesson for your new job!"

She rushed out the door and we could hear her start down the steps. We had only a second before my brother, David, appeared at the door, grinning from ear to ear.

"Guess you fuckin' hippies are going to have to clean up your acts, a little!"

He quickly pulled the door shut in time to block the slipper I threw at his head and retreated down the hall, laughing loudly all the way.

"Damn! This was a nice quiet day until they all came home," Joe mumbled as he pulled together a pile of sheets and pillowcases.

* * *

I had been working as a busboy at the Lotus Room, a Chinese restaurant, for a few weeks when I received a call from Betsy Hess, a fellow Walther Leaguer I had met at the Houston retreat the previous spring. Betsy was in a pickle. She had accepted the Walther League's offer to become a regional staffer after she had applied to the united Presbyterian Church in the USA to be part of an international "Youth and World Crisis Seminar" that was going to be touring six different cities over three months, beginning in March. She had not heard from the Presbyterians and thought her application had not been accepted, so she had taken the Walther League job. Now the Presbyterians had notified her that she was accepted. She couldn't take on both assignments. She had called Frieda to discuss her dilemma and learned that I had graduated early. She was calling to see if I could substitute for her in the Youth and World Crisis Seminar, beginning almost immediately!

I couldn't believe that yet more good fortune was coming my way. After an intense few days of phone calls involving Presbyterians, Lutherans and, of course, my parents, I was accepted as one of six North Americans who joined nine youth from countries around the globe to make up the Youth and World Crisis Seminar. I had no idea what exactly would be expected of me as a seminar participant, but I happily quit the Lotus Room and flew to Cincinnati on March 2 for a two-week orientation.

I was met at the airport in Cincinnati by the Reverend Kyoji Buma, executive secretary for the Office of Youth Relations of the United Presbyterian Church in the USA and the visionary behind the seminar. This unassuming leader was the first of four pastors I would meet over the course of the seminar who would, in several separate, deep conversations, both challenge and support me in finalizing my decision to resist the draft.

Kyoji, as he insisted we call him, was a self-described "missionary to the U.S.A. from Japan" and had been working in New York City at the headquarters of the World Council of Churches (WCC) for nearly a decade. He told me that he had originally gotten connected to the WCC by participating in a summer work camp in Nagasaki repairing damage from the atomic bomb dropped there by the United States in 1945. He had then been selected to study at Yale Divinity School, returned as a pastor to his hometown of Kyoto, and then was convinced to return to the States and work for the WCC. In his current position, he led the youth work of the Presbyterian Church nationally and chaired the World Council for Christian Education. He said he was an admirer of the new Walther League and asked me a ton of questions as we drove from the airport to Wildwood, a Presbyterian retreat center in 375 acres of woods in the hills outside of Cincinnati.

I was among the last to arrive, as most of the kids who traveled internationally had come in over the weekend, and it was now lunch time on Monday. I was shown to one of the dorm-style rooms and introduced to Eduardo, my roommate from Ecuador, who spoke very little English—matching my lack of proficiency in Spanish. We sorted out how we would share the room with a lot of pointing and saying "OK? OK," to each other, and then walked outside a short distance to the dining hall. There, I was introduced to the 13 other young people—we were all between the ages of 17 and 22—as well as the adult chaperones for the two-week orientation, Lyn and Jean Larson, a married couple from Minnesota who had recently returned from a three-year assignment as development staff for the United Methodist church in Algiers, Algeria.

During that first meal and continuing into the afternoon and evening, I remember feeling completely overwhelmed and totally outside of my comfort zone. I had never met a person from another country other than Canada and Mexico, and now here, in the course of a few minutes, I had met kids from Japan, Poland, Finland, Iran, Ghana, Bolivia, Ecuador, Indonesia—and a couple who had just returned from living in Algeria! Additionally, half of the North Americans were Black kids from Memphis and Washington, D.C., and the other two whites were from Des Moines. Sitting there, I was sure that my invitation must have been a mistake and as soon as Kyoji figured out I didn't belong, he would send me back to St. Louis!

My anxieties were relieved over the subsequent hours, and then days, of the orientation, as Kyoji, Lyn, and Jean expertly facilitated our introductions to each other and our development as a team. We listened to and learned from each other in a wide variety of ways. Some of the leadership activities—like public speaking and improvisation skits—were similar to experiences I had had with the Walther League Leadership Institute the previous summer. Kyoji had planned that our group would be split into three teams of five and sent to three different cities after orientation, so we spent a fair amount of time practicing presenting panel discussions on a range of current topics in various combinations of five. Looking back on it now, I believe part of what Jean, Lyn, and Kyoji were doing, especially during the second week, was evaluating various dynamics and balance that were created by these different combinations.

Several times over the course of the two weeks in Wildwood, I had the opportunity to have in-depth conversations with either Lyn and Jean—separately and together; in those conversations, I heard many more details about their time in Algeria than they had shared with the entire group. What impressed me most about them was their deep commitment to the work they were doing and the people they were serving in Algeria, and, as part of that, their support of the revolutionary nationalist government there. Even as the government's policies changed, growing more restrictive of foreign nationals' (especially those affiliated with Christian organizations) ability to work and move about the country, they did not become critical of the government. They felt that their work spoke of their Christian beliefs, and they did not proselytize. As we talked about Vietnam, the draft, and my potential resistance, what stuck with me about the conversations we had was how committed Jean and Lyn were to living their beliefs—and living with the consequences. I experienced them as living role models: dedicated Christian activists whose work in the broader movement for social change was a true "calling ; they were willing to risk losing, at a minimum, access to conventional, middle-class measures of success. Their love for each other and their shared beliefs sustained them—and inspired me to think that what I was contemplating doing as a draft resister would not stop me from having a happy, fulfilled life.

Our orientation session at Wildwood ended on Friday, March 13, when we were given our team and city assignments for the remaining two months of the seminar. I was assigned to go to Peoria, Illinois and Birmingham, Alabama with Joe King from Memphis, TN, Yoko Tomiyana from Tokyo, Japan, Elizabeth Jastrzebowska from Warsaw, Poland, and Linda Salazar from Cochabanba, Bolivia. The entire seminar group would reassemble in one month in Louisville, Kentucky for a week's break for reflection and any needed assignment changes. Then, after our second month, we would be together for one final week in Chicago during the Presbyterian Church's national convention. We would be presented to the convention delegates, and Kyoji would give them a brief report on the seminar.

My group and I flew to Peoria first and were met by our host, Pastor George Hirst, and our adult coordinators, David and DeDee Jensen. George was a tall, thin man of about 50; he was pastor of the United Church of Christ congregation in East Peoria and led the Metropolitan Ministry Team, an ecumenical group of clergy from Peoria and the surrounding communities. David and DeDee were in their late 20s and were recently returned Peace Corps volunteers who, like Lyn and Jean, had been hired by the seminar to provide logistical support and supervision to the five of us while we were in Peoria.

George was as high-strung and driven as David and DeDee had been laid-back and mellow. George saw our seminar team as a catalyst for engaging young people from the area in the world's problems, trying to move what he saw as a very conservative rural area into a more open, understanding, and supportive community that would address the crises of racism and poverty. On pretty much each of the next 28 days we would spend in the area, George had scheduled a minimum of one presentation for us in one of the local churches, service clubs such as Kiwanis and 4-H, or high school classes, as well as radio and TV appearances. We had presentations in nearly every small town surrounding Peoria: Morton, Chillicothe, Pekin, East Peoria. Often, when we were appearing at a high school, we would lead discussions in six or seven classes over the course of the day, so that by the end of our time in Peoria we had made a total of 73 presentations.

After the first 10 or 15 presentations, we became a fairly synchronized and effective team of presenters. Typically, we would have about an hour for a session, and we would spend about 20 minutes presenting and 40 minutes in dialogue with our audience. Each of us combined some aspect of our personal story with some type of position statement on an issue or two. Most of the people we interacted with were from very small towns and farms; most people had some connection to farming or working for Caterpillar. There was a great deal of interest in hearing from Yoko, Linda and Elizabeth—and less interest in hearing from Joe and me—for most of our audiences. While the "Midwestern polite" culture prevailed overall, I remember many of the discussions becoming quite heated around Vietnam, race relations, socialism (because of Elizabeth, who described herself as a Catholic Socialist and vigorously debated all comers), and pacifism (mainly because of Yoko and only sometimes because of me). Depending on the audience, we would talk more or less about our Christian faith—often in response to audience questions.

While George did not attend all our presentations, he did come to many, especially those in churches. He would listen carefully during the sessions and never participate since he wanted to make sure that we and the teens who attended our presentations had all the "airtime." Afterward, however, he would ask us all many questions about what we had said, trying to get a deeper understanding of what we meant or what experience we had had that led us to saying what we said. When I had the opportunity, I sought him out for more conversation, especially around issues of conscience, social change and, of course, my continued wrestling with resistance to the draft.

George was just a few years younger than my father, and I realize now that he gave the me the kind of attention, positive feedback, and acceptance that I was missing from my father. George also pushed me to clarify my thinking and to be able to articulate clear, concrete reasons that draft resistance made sense to me. He was very pragmatic in his own work, focused much more on the logistics and mechanics of getting a food bank organized or having great turnout at one of our presentations. He said that maybe it came from being brought up on a farm, but after thinking about things for a while and getting as clear as he could, he felt that he needed to take action—some concrete step or steps—in order to get to any further or deeper understanding of a problem.

And so, a few weeks into my time in Peoria—on Maundy Thursday of Holy Week—I acted. I sent the following letter to my family:

March 26, 1970

Dear Loving parents, brothers, sisters, all:

I am writing this letter not to tell you of the external events that have been happening here in Peoria, but of internal thoughts and dreams that have been in my head for many months that have culminated into a decision in the past few days. Because the time is now short until my eighteenth birthday, I decided that I had to weigh the pros and cons for a final time and make a decision as to how I am going to deal with the draft. I have made that decision and it is to resist, to refuse to register.

I think the main reason I really made my decision this week is because it is Holy Week, a week of tremendous meaning to me. It has great meaning to me because during this week many, many years ago, a man named Jesus Christ made a decision—a decision to confront the community of Jews that had gathered in Jerusalem with his radical beliefs as to how people must live if they are to be righteous and godly. I feel that on Palm Sunday as Jesus rode into Jerusalem, he knew that the majority of the people there would not agree with him and would probably execute him. But He knew He had to do it—that the time is now, for if not now, when? So, Jesus did confront the people with His love and His freedom and His saying to them that they must try to live like Him and believe in Him as the Truth if they were to have eternal life. He did this and was killed for it by the Establishment of his time. Rulers of all times can and will not tolerate free and loving men—they are powerful threats to the oppression the tyrants represent. But the important thing is that Jesus rose on Easter Sunday proving that he was God and that the things he talked about—loving, being free, caring about others—always will rise and conquer.

This is where I find my hope that love will conquer hate and life will conquer death. And let me say at this point, and let it be perfectly clear, that I do not consider myself to be a Christ figure or a martyr of any kind, but I am a Christian and therefore feel I must act according to Christian ethics such as "Thou shalt not kill" and "Love thy neighbor as thyself." I feel that my decision is a Christian decision made by my Christian conscience.

I know that we have discussed my reasons for taking this action before, but I will endeavor to write them down here as clearly as possible so that perhaps they will become more clear in your mind.

First of all, the purpose of the draft is quite clear to me. On one hand, it takes mainly the poor and oppressed young people of this society to kill other people that the "leaders" of this nation feel must be oppressed and, on the other hand, takes mainly the middle and upper class young people and channels them into situations such as college or occupations such as defense plant work where they can get deferments and be spared the dirty work of killing and being killed. In short, it forces all young people (men rather) to either support the militaristic death machine that this country is fast becoming or to go to jail or into exile if they can't, in good conscience, support it. And I cannot conscientiously support such a coercive system that is contrary to both traditional American freedom and the Christian ethic of love.

Secondly, the draft blatantly symbolizes and, in fact, is a part of the sick values that control this country, values that it seems the majority of Americans believe in and will go to any means to defend. That is, the value of property, material wealth and pure, unadulterated selfishness versus the value of human beings, being human, and selflessness.

I cannot say that I believe in love, humanness, giving and sharing, and support such a hate-filled, inhumane, selfish, I-come-first system. I cannot say I am opposed to the war and the draft and still support them with my body, my mind, and my actions. In short, I cannot be a hypocrite and support a system that enslaves and oppresses people all over the world, people who are my brothers, and I can't support a system that would enslave and oppress me. I must be free from anything or anybody who would not let me act in a loving, human, moral way.

So, I feel I must commit myself to changing this death-oriented society and I have to do that with my life. I have to confront the community and the power structure with what they are doing and I want to make them think 'why.' Because if they think why, I know that if they are really human, they will change. And I think that my 18th birthday is perhaps the first time I can stand up and say "Look!" and "Why? and "It can be better" in a really big way. The draft gives me a choice, a clear-cut choice, as to choose to support the death-destruction system or choose a life of loving creativity.

I choose the latter one.

And for me, the threat of a certain jail sentence and repercussions of that are offset by the vision I have as to how life should be lived—loving, justly, peacefully, freely—and my commitment to living that vision.

And finally, I know that this is very hard for you all to accept and I'm sure it will get much harder sooner than we really want. But these are times when we must take a stand and, relatively, the hardships we all will suffer a little compared to the Vietnamese, the Mexican-Americans, the poor Blacks, the poor Whites, the Bolivian Indians, the American Indians and all the other people on the hurting end of America's death-stick.

I do not say you must agree with me, but I only wish that you might understand that I must do what I must do, and that I am acting out of Christian conscience. I must be a free man. I must be a loving man. I must act and commit my whole life to the betterment of my brothers. I therefore cannot support a system that is completely against all these things: not at all, not with one grain of sand.

In the strength and the hope of the Resurrection,

Paul

I remember the moments after finishing the letter: sitting silently late that night at a desk in a stranger's house in Chillicothe, reading all six pages of it over again, then folding it carefully and sealing it in an envelope addressed to my parents. I felt the full weight of my decision and its implications for my family and me. I worried about what impact my letter and my actual non-registration would have on my parents, especially my father. I licked a stamp and put it on the envelope, then turned out the light. Moonlight shone faintly through the thin curtains as I stripped off my clothes and crawled under the sheets of the creaky guest bed. I was doing it! It felt right! I would be a resister, I thought, smiling just a little as I turned over and fell asleep.

* * *

Within the next week, I had written a similar letter expressing my decision addressed to my Walther League colleagues and sent it to Pat Krause at headquarters in Chicago, asking that she make copies and distribute it to the Walther League council, trustees, current staff and staff who were going to be joining as full-time staffers—as I would—on July 1. We would all be meeting in Rosebud, South Dakota, at the end of April for our next council meeting and to finalize the plans for our next national convention that would take place in Rosebud in mid-August. I also shared my decision with Lyn and Jean and the rest of the Youth and World Crisis Seminar when we gathered in Louisville for our one-week break. I was feeling relieved about making the decision and excited, now, to plan how to make a public statement of my resistance.

In Louisville, our teams were reshuffled a bit and, in our case, Joe and Elizabeth left us and we were joined by Patricia, from Washington, D.C., and Raphy, from Indonesia. We flew to Birmingham on April 18 and were met by Drake Whitelow, a young woman who worked for the Episcopalian Diocese of Birmingham and served as our local coordinator, as well as logistics manager. While we did not have a busy schedule of presentations in Birmingham, we had the opportunity to get a very in-depth feel for being in the deep South. We went to Selma and Montgomery, seeing firsthand many of the sites of key civil rights marches and meetings in those two towns as well as Birmingham, and meeting with members and leaders of the Black faith community.

Because our schedule was much less demanding than in Peoria, I had more time to spend with my host families in Birmingham. This was quite a contrasting cultural experience for me, as I spent about a third of my time there with the Lalor family in a very wealthy neighborhood of Birmingham. Mr. Lalor was retired from the U.S. Navy, where he had been an officer on a nuclear submarine; he was now working as an executive vice president for the local power company. Mrs. Lalor did not work outside of the home, and they had two sons, one in middle school and the other in high school. We had long, somewhat contentious—but very polite—discussions over dinner about the war in Vietnam and the role of the military in society.

In contrast, I spent the remainder of my time in a middle-class Black neighborhood of Birmingham with the Davis family. Mr. Davis owned a service station and Mrs. Davis was a schoolteacher. They had been directly involved in the civil rights movement, going back to the late-1930s; they told me how their neighborhood was known as "Dynamite Hill" because of all the bombings that had taken place when Black families began moving into the neighborhood in the 1950s. The Davises had raised four children in those tumultuous times. One of those children, Angela, was now a very prominent and controversial philosophy instructor and political activist in California who would later that year be indicted as a co-conspirator in a major criminal case involving an attempt to free Black Panther George Jackson from a courtroom shootout (she would be acquitted). The Davises were, like Lyn and Jean, inspirational to me in terms of living their convictions, in their case, over a long period of time. Seeing their life together each day, I could imagine a future for myself living out a lifetime commitment to the struggle for social justice that would require sacrifices but could be sustained. I remember feeling confident, affirmed and supported in my recent decision to resist the draft by the living example of the Davises.

* * *

But just six weeks later in Chicago, I wasn't feeling either confident or supported about being a draft resister. I was plagued by self-doubt once again. And now it was only three weeks until my eighteenth birthday.

And yet, at this moment, instead of obsessing, I was getting a lesson. I was sitting on the edge of Joe King's bed next to Jeff, giving all my attention to what was happening on the street seven stories below us. We were in the huge YMCA residence hotel kitty-corner on Wabash from the Hilton. All of us from Youth and World Crisis were staying at the Y while most of the convention delegates—and the convention meetings—were across the street at the Hilton.

"See, look now. He's movin' on him, makin' his play."

We could see the middle-aged white man in the short sleeves and skinny tie turn toward the young Black man who had just walked up to him and smile. They began talking while waiting for the light to change.

"You mark my word. They'll cross, stop, talk some more. Then walk back and head over to the park."

And that was exactly what happened over the next couple of minutes. This was the third or fourth time we had watched the scene unfold in the past 20 minutes. Joe was teaching Jeff and me about the street hustle for blow jobs.

"Joe, how come you know all about this stuff, man?" I had missed hanging out with Joe since our team had been shuffled, and he was now hanging out with Jeff since they had spent the last month together in Pittsburgh.

"Man, you know we have a bunch of church meetings in Memphis. I learned firsthand," Joe replied.

"You do this hustle?"

"I watched it, at least. You know, when you need money you do what you have to. These white preachers, man, they sex-crazed." We laughed and watched the men on the corner. Once you saw the patterns of interaction and understood the code, it was hard to stop seeing the transactions. I had never imagined that this all could be taking place outside a church convention. Joe had laughed at my naiveté.

"You guys going to go to the service tonight?" I asked.

"What service is that?"

I passed over a flyer that I had picked up earlier in the day from a table in one of the breakout sessions on combating world hunger. It said that there would be a service and celebration of the Eucharist conducted by something called the "Underground Church" beginning at 10 that evening.

"If this is the same Underground Church that showed up in Denver last year at the Lutheran convention I went to, it should be pretty good. They had good music and Malcolm Boyd preached," I said.

Joe looked at me. "Naw, I think I will pass. I am going to go hit some clubs around here, I think. There is some good blues and stuff. We have to go to that closing service on Sunday, right? I think that is enough church for me."

"Who else is going?" Jeff asked. "I mean, maybe if Linda or Paula or someone, you know, goes."

"Yeah, he knows. You fellas got the same thing on your mind as those preachers out there do!" Joe nodded toward the street. We all laughed, knowing Joe was on target.

"Well, you boys get on outta here and let me get ready to go out my own self. You sort out that church shit yourselves," Joe said, laughing.

Jeff and I squeezed out of the narrow room into the hallway. Jeff said he wanted to go to his room for a little while, but he would meet me in the Y's lobby at 9:45 and we could walk over together. I agreed and headed to my own room, since it was only a little past 8 p.m. I grabbed my journal off the desk, flicked on the light, and flopped on the bed. I paged back to my entries from early April, when I had been so certain and had made my decision to resist. I paged forward, scanning my entries over the past six weeks or so, reflecting on all that had happened and trying to understand why I had begun to doubt my decision not to register.

So much had happened in such a short period: President Nixon and Secretary of State Kissinger had escalated the war by invading Cambodia with U.S. troops on April 28; then, within a week, National Guard troops shot and killed four students s at Kent State University in Ohio and two students at Jackson State University in Mississippi. A wave of student-led strikes then shut down hundreds of campuses and huge protests against the war and the killings took place across the country. While the invasion and massive air bombing campaign continued unabated at this point, Nixon had publicly announced that the troops would be withdrawn from Cambodia "soon," as they had allegedly accomplished their mission of destroying North Vietnamese bases. any of the college campuses remained closed, some administrators making the decision not to resume classes until the fall semester.

During much of the first week after the Cambodian invasion and at the time of the Kent State shooting, I had been, first, driving from Chicago to the Native American reservation in Rosebud, South Dakota and then, meeting there for two days with all of the new Walther League staffers. We were joined by the new executive director, Mark Hellman, as well as the current staff and Youth Council members who were planning what would be our next national convention in August at the tribal campground on the reservation. We had had very little access to national news but based on the facts we had coming into the meeting in Rosebud and what we gathered from radio newscasts, our collective mood reflected a new sense of seriousness, immediacy, and urgency related to everything we were doing. It felt, even in that remote corner of the country, that the nation was coming apart at the seams. Somehow, we, in the large, vaguely defined amalgam of a social and cultural movement, were being called upon to act to stop what we saw as our country blundering its way toward death, destruction, and oblivion.

Since I believed that my public act of resistance by not registering for the draft on my birthday would, almost certainly, lead to my arrest and imprisonment, I began, anew, to question the effectiveness and impact of such an individual act. I raised these questions with some staff, like Pat Krause, whom I had known for more than a year, and others, like Debbie Sweet and Sue LaPorte, whom I had just met—all to no new resolution. Then, I had the opportunity to stop off in St. Louis for about 30 hours on my way back to Birmingham from Chicago, and saw my parents, my sister Susie, and Joe and Dennis. Again, I found no respite from my questions about effectiveness and impact—and instead added more unresolved issues to my mind as I had conversations with my parents and got a better sense of how worried they were becoming about me the closer it got to my birthday.

So, now, here I was in Chicago, a little less than three weeks from my birthday, in a dinky room in a funky YMCA, no closer to clarity. I had not made any formal changes to my plans for a public non-registration act or set of acts at the state or Missouri District of the Lutheran Church-Missouri Synod's convention that would take place in St. Louis the week of my birthday. But, I knew in my heart of hearts that I was not fully committed to the action now. I had no idea what I was going to do. I dropped my journal onto the floor, turned over to face the wall, and pulled the thin pillow over my head.

I woke with a start and looked at my watch and shouted "Shit! Shit! Shit!" It was just about 9:45 and was supposed to be in the lobby to meet Jeff. I slammed out of my room, stopped briefly at the bathroom on the way to the elevator and waited, it seemed like forever, for one of the four elevators that serviced the dozen floors and probably 200 rooms to come. Finally, I got to the lobby and saw Jeff slouched in a chair in the corner. I quickly walked over.

"Sorry, man, sorry! Look, I fell asleep, but I think we won't miss much if we head over right now."

"Oh, man, don't worry. I was nodding here myself. Look, man, before we go, I got somethin' for you to, ah, you know, make the service more interesting."

He stood up and opened his clenched left fist palm side up, revealing a broken half-tablet of something!

"What the heck?"

"It's mesc, man. I took the other half and I've had some from this batch before. It's cool. It's pretty mellow, nothin' to worry about."

I had taken mescaline once before at a Christmas Eve service the previous year. I knew it could be hallucinogenic but I had half a tab then, too, and it made me feel alert, noticing things about the music and making colors more intense. I remember thinking that somehow it couldn't hurt me and might make me feel better, so I grabbed it out of Jeff's hand and popped it into my mouth.

"OK, man, thanks. Now, let's get moving over to the Hilton!"

We walked rapidly across the nearly empty lobby and out the doors onto Wabash Avenue and up to the corner where we had seen—from Joe's window—the hustlers and conventioneers connect. I looked around as we waited for the light to change, wondering if Jeff and I looked like marks to anyone. Nothing happened except the light changed and we walked across the street, entered the Hilton and found our way to the elevators. As we were walking, I fished the crinkled flyer out of my back pocket and found the name of the ballroom we were trying to find. We went up to the mez-zanine level and wandered around for a while until we heard guitars and voices.

We followed the music a few hundred feet into a ballroom that was dimly lit, primarily by many candles burning brightly on a table set in the middle of a few rows of chairs arranged in a semi-circle. We found our way over to a couple of empty chairs toward the back and sat down. Glancing around the room, I didn't see anyone I knew. A young man with long brown hair had noticed us when we came in and now came up to us and gave us each a set of mimeographed papers that had been stapled together and pointed to the bottom of the first page. We nodded our heads and joined in the responsive reading.

The mescaline started kicking in. What I remember next is a long period—it seemed like hours but probably was 15 or 20 minutes—when I became acutely aware of the candles and candlelight, with human voices fading into the background, almost as a hum that somehow was modulating in rhythm with the flickering and dancing of the candles themselves. I was completely absorbed, losing myself in the light, feeling calm, alone, and yet connected to the others in the service in a very vague, distant manner.

Suddenly, the energy shifted in the room and I remember being pulled back into a focus on the two pastors—a man and a woman in colorful robes and clerical collars—as they prepared for sharing the Eucharist. Their excitement and enthusiasm was palpable to me in my heightened state and I felt myself being drawn into the pastors' words about life, death, sharing, community, and everlasting peace, actually experiencing the words as feelings, as having a real, palpable meaning to me and the questions I had been wrestling with.

I joined in the line going up to the pastors to receive the bread and wine. The acoustic guitars seemed amplified to me, as did the voices around me, singing the communion hymn, "Allelu! Allelu! The Lord has risen, it is true, everybody sing Allelu!" People began rocking, swaying to the rhythm as the line inched forward. After receiving the bread and wine, a few folks began forming into some kind of conga line, and as others joined, it grew and snaked its way throughout the room in a mixture of singing, laughing and shouting. After my turn receiving communion, I turned around, looked for Jeff, and could not see him anywhere. At that moment, a girl with a flashing smile and short black hair grabbed my hand and put my hands on her shoulders; I followed her into the shimmering, shaking line that now had at least 100 people in it.

The dancing, singing, and clapping continued for at least 10 or 15 minutes after everyone who wanted to had taken the bread and wine. At some point, the pastors ended the service with a blessing and a call for everyone to exchange greetings—hugs, kisses, handshakes—of peace. As I made my way, hugging and greeting people who were complete strangers to me, I remember a feeling of intense connection with each person I met, a feeling that I could be asked for anything from any one of them and I would willingly give it—and that, likewise, I could get anything I needed from anyone in the room. I knew, simply *knew* on some visceral level, that we were all bonded together in a community and that the glue, the spirit that held us all together and was greater than all of us combined, that insisted we care about each other and about all the strangers in the world, was what I knew and worshipped as God.

Everything was so clear to me in those moments right after the service. I felt that I knew what I had to do, now, that resistance to the draft was definitely my path forward. I experienced this as an affirmation of community and life, an act of my faith much more than as a political action that had to have clear political impact. The impact I was seeking and seeing that I could have was that of being aligned with the demands of my own conscience, what I understood that my faith required of me in the time and place I was living. Nothing more and, importantly, nothing less.

I finally found Jeff, and we worked our way through the thinning crowd and eventually made our way out of the Hilton and onto Michigan Avenue. It was a little after midnight. Somehow, we safely navigated the streets of Chicago's South Loop over the next five-plus hours, finding our way in and out of all-night diners, our rooms at the Y, wandering the streets and eventually ending up at Monroe Harbor and Lake Michigan just before sunrise.

As we sat down on the concrete piling alongside the lake, the horizon was just a shade lighter than the inky black of the lake's surface. Slowly, the sky lightened. Gray clouds began showing a pink tinge and, ever so slowly, the red, then orange, then yellow, orb of the sun was drawn into the eastern sky and the lake turned blue in celebration of the new day. We two snoozed alongside the harbor until the combination of traffic noise from Lake Shore Drive and a cold stiffness from the cement we were sitting on motivated us to find our way back to the Y, where we slept the day away.

CHAPTER 5:
INTO THE RESISTANCE

"**O**h, my God, it's the Feds!"

Jane sounded the alarm from her place on the large, worn couch that faced the bay windows in the living room at the front of the McPherson House, the commune that she, Dennis, their infant son Justin, and about 10 other adults lived in on the west side of St. Louis. It was Tuesday evening, June 9, and we had just started the planning meeting to finalize our activities at the Missouri District Lutheran convention at the seminary the next week, ahead of my draft resistance action on the final day of the convention.

I turned around in my chair that was just in front of the windows and looked out as Jane walked over to me. "Go upstairs, Paul! Go to our room! We'll handle this!"

I squinted to make sure of what I thought was true was true as the two white, middle-aged men in coats and ties started walking up the sidewalk to the front steps.

"No, no, it's OK, really! I know those two. They are from the church. That is Pastor Mensing with the beard and, oh, yeah, Pastor Jones! Man, I haven't seen him since eighth grade!"

"Well, what the fuck! Why are they wearing ties to this fucking meeting—" Jane began laughing.

"And what does he have in his hands?" I asked

"Weird. I have no idea."

Jane and I walked into the hallway as the doorbell rang. We could see the two pastors through the glass door windows. I pulled the door open.

"Pastor Mensing! Pastor Jones! Welcome, welcome. It's great to see you both! Please come in and meet my friends. This is Jane Cummins."

Jane shook their hands and showed them into the living room, where everyone else was standing now. They made their way around the room, shaking hands with each person. As the introductions were being made, I was eyeing the large metal object in Joe Mensing's left hand. It was about two feet long and seemed to be some kind of metal cylinder, but it wasn't solid; it had been carved somehow. The two men sat on the couch, and I sat down next to them.

"Sorry we were late. We got turned around a little on the one-way streets. It's been a while since I've been in this area," Pastor Mensing said.

"No problem. We had just started talking when we saw you walk up together."

"Well, Paul, as long as we disrupted the meeting, let me continue to disrupt a little. You are probably wondering what the hell this is!" Pastor Mensing lifted the metal cylinder up and showed it to everyone. "This is a birthday present for you. It's an artillery shell casing. See here is the base, and you can see I have used a torch and cut into it." He pointed to two large peace symbols cut out on one side of the shell and then traced his fingers around the abstract patterns he had cut into the rest of the casing.

"I am making these to 'beat swords into ploughshares,' as the Scripture says. It's a candle holder now, and I hope you enjoy it, that it gives you peace, as you are trying to wage peace with your brave act of draft resistance."

I was totally overwhelmed by this unexpected gift, as well as Pastor Mensing's generous words of support for me. I could only croak out a few words of thanks in response, leaving me feeling totally inadequate as the transformed shell casing was passed from person to person around the room. My friends more than made up for me as they heaped praise on the pastor's artistry, as well as his generosity. As Jane facilitated the segue and brought us back to crafting a plan for our activities at the convention, I let myself sink into a sense of being surrounded by a community of friends committed to a purpose that was much larger than each of us. It was a peaceful start to what promised to be one of the most intense weeks of my life.

* * *

They stood in absolute silence—10 from our group dressed in black, their expressionless faces painted white. They stood in a straight line directly across the narrow street from the entrance to the seminary's chapel, where the opening service was taking place. I stood on the other side of the street right outside the double doors that led into the chapel. I listened as the faint organ music drifted into the summer evening. Soon the doors would open and the convention delegates, church officials and their families would come flooding out into the summer evening expecting, perhaps, to linger in the twilight and chat pleasantly about the service or the convention sessions starting in the morning.

Instead, we would be confronting them with a stark reminder of the war 7,000 miles away: a specter of death right in front of them. And I would be passing out my personal statement of draft resistance entitled "Here I stand: I can do no other," a direct quote from Martin Luther. It was minutes away from happening and I could feel the sweat bead up and then run down my back as my stomach tightened. I was excited, on edge—at once both elated and terrified. My resistance was becoming a reality.

Jane stood in the center of the group with a three-by-three poster-board sign that read: STOP THE WAR! hanging from a thick string around her neck, a candle cradled in a paper cup in each hand. The rest of the group had candles at the ready; they would be holding the candles chest high to illuminate their starkly painted faces. I listened closely and heard what I knew was the recessional hymn, because I had managed to get my hands on a service program—thanks to my mother, who—as part of our church's Altar Guild—had volunteered to set up for communion at the convention's opening service. I waved over to the group, and they lit their candles quickly and then reassembled their line. I admired them briefly, thinking they did, indeed, look quite eerie in the gathering twilight. Then the double doors burst open and Pastor Scherer, president of the Missouri District, walked out and peered out from the top of the steps at Jane and the group.

"Oh, for the love of Pete!" he growled, spinning around in a flash of flowing white robes, to face the congregation that was following him, singing as the organ boomed. He ignored me, standing at the foot of the stairs with my mimeographed statement held out to him. I waited and watched as he greeted worshippers as they exited, shaking hands, saying "Christ's peace!" and occasionally making small talk with those he must have known.

As people passed President Scherer and moved toward the stairs, they looked across the street and paused, falling silent for a moment as they took in the spectacle and read the sign. I took advantage of their momentary confusion and pushed my flyer with my statement in their direction, saying variations of "Peace be with you!" or "Peace, now!" Most took the flyer and walked rapidly away. A few paused, read the headline from Martin Luther and a few lines of my statement, before they, too, walked off. A handful walked across the street and up to our line of protesters and stared, tried to engage them in conversation or made rude comments. All were met with silence, and they left after a few minutes.

The crowd thinned out rapidly—much more quickly, I thought, than most did after services in my experience. Pastor Scherer was still standing just inside the doorway, talking quietly to a small knot of men gathered around him. I had a handful of flyers left and thought, "What the heck?"

and started up the stairs toward him and his group. At that moment, my mother came out the side door carrying a large box of Eucharist-related materials that she was going to return to Concordia in Maplewood.

"Paul!" she shouted across the corridor, and I turned and took a few steps toward her.

"What a great protest! They look great!" she said, nodding toward Jane and the group. "I am SO proud of you!" she continued as she turned to walk to the parking lot.

"Thanks, Mom!" I said and turned back toward the spot where Pastor Scherer had been standing. He and his group of aides (or whatever they were) had hurried back into the chapel, the doors shutting behind them. I felt relieved that I wouldn't have to talk to him right then. I took a deep breath as I turned back toward Jane and the rest of the group.

"Ok, I think we are done here!" Jane blew her candles out, as did the rest of the group members.

"That was so cool!" somebody, I think Ann, said from the group. "But weird, weird and hard to stay in character or whatever."

"Hard to be dead, huh?" Joe's voice cracked from the back of the group that was now slowly meandering toward our cars in the parking lot. "Here, have one of these and it'll come quicker and easier, maybe." He held up a pack of cigarettes, shook one out and lit it.

Everyone laughed and the relief spread through us. The first act was over, I thought, and had gone pretty well.

Ten minutes later, our four-car caravan rolled into the parking lot behind Luther Memorial. Pastor Trautmann was standing outside the side doors that led to the church's large meeting room below the sanctuary. His daughter, Claudia—along with two other church members, John Bringewatt and Leon Williams—was a member of our St. Louis Hunger Team. Together, they had prevailed on the pastor and the church's council to allow us to use Luther Memorial as a sort of headquarters for our loosely organized coalition of young people attending the convention. In addition to the Hunger Team, our coalition included local members of the Black Youth Unlimited and the Draft Resistance Action Group that we had founded the week before with Pastors Mensing and Jones. Mark Hellman, the new executive director of the Walther League and Dan Gilbert, the new youth staffer who would take over the Central and Southern Plains Region from Frieda, were there as well. Dan had brought a handful of League members from his Kansas City congregation along.

"Welcome! WELCOME!" Pastor Trautmann called out as we piled out of the cars and he yanked the hefty wooden door open. "Right down the stairs, there, some of your friends are already here. There are cool drinks on the counter! Welcome! Welcome!"

He followed us down the stairs into the brightly lit church basement. I knew most of the about 15 kids milling around there. Dennis was in the back of the room sitting on a couch, nestling Justin in his arms, trying to keep him from fully waking up in the buzz of excited voices, laughter and scraping chairs as we grabbed drinks and joined the others around a group of tables that had been formed into a large rectangle. Pastor Trautmann quickly quieted the group and got everyone's attention, seemingly without any effort.

"I want to welcome you all again to Luther Memorial," he said. "We are pleased to provide hospitality and a respite place for you as you attend the convention this week and do the Lord's work. I know it is not easy, this work to heal our broken world from the sins of war, racism and hunger, but our Lord shows us the way". He went on and on, moving through what amounted to a short sermon and then into an itemization of the rules we were to follow while staying in the church basement and using the kitchen. I was kind of surprised that he was going over all of this. We had provided all the information to convention coalition members in writing already, but I guessed he just had to be sure. I looked around the room and nobody seemed upset, just a little bored.

"OK, OK. Well, I know you had a big night tonight with the opening service, and I have to say that I was impressed," he said as he finally seemed to be wrapping up. "I think you really shook people up that came out of that service, reminded them that our church is in this world and has to help heal this world. Anyway, I thank you and I am sure others will thank you this week. God bless and rest well. I'll see you tomorrow!"

I stood up and shook Pastor Trautmann's hand as he moved toward the door to exit. I turned back to everyone. "Uh, well, thanks for being here, everybody," I said. "We don't really need to have a meeting right now, unless you guys want to or have questions or something. We are going to have breakfast right here at 7:30 and anyone who is not staying here"—I looked at John, Claudia and Darrell—"is welcome to join us. We'll go over what is planned for the day each morning at breakfast, OK? So, I mean, if there are questions … otherwise, we can just hang out and stuff, or go to sleep."

"Yeah, I got a question, man." It was Nick from Black Youth Unlimited, who shifted around in his chair and looked me in the eye. "What the hell did you do to your hair, man? I didn't recognize your ass when you came in here with the pastor!" Everyone roared in laughter and I turned beet red.

"Ahh, man, you know, I want these people to listen to the message, not get hung up on—"

"Your hair?" Nick interrupted. "Your hair and my skin, no matter what we do, they not likely to listen, you know."

"Well, but, I'm trying, just like, to not meet their mental image of a draft dodger."

"You know I'm just playin' with ya, right? Yeah, I guess you gotta try, but, damn, boy, you didn't have to cut it ALL off like that."

With that, Nick pushed his bulk out of the folding chair and walked over to me and put out his hand. We shook some version of the black power handshake. I felt very self-conscious for a second until Nick grinned and said. "Lighten up, man, you gonna be all right. Nobody is gonna arrest you and take you to jail any time soon for this draft thing." He let go of my hand and put his hand on my shoulder to turn me away from the table and the others, who were now scooting back their chairs and getting up. He nodded toward the kitchen. "You got something we can snack on in there? I'm starved." We spent the next half hour eating ice cream and talking over plans for the convention.

* * *

Over the next two days and nights of the convention, I rode a roller coaster of emotions. They ranged from the highs of excitement about my upcoming public act of resistance and my sense of community and connection with my friends and supporters at Luther Memorial to the lows brought about by the tedium of listening to endless convention debates about what seemed like irrelevant issues.

My friends and I maintained a constant presence throughout the convention by staffing a booth in the seminary gymnasium where the plenary sessions took place. With our flyers, colorful posters and copies of *Bridge*—the Walther League's monthly newspaper—we eagerly sought to engage the delegates in discussions about the issues of the day, including my draft resistance. I had forgotten my observations from attending other church conventions that most delegates simply wanted to get business done quickly and get on to socializing with their friends. Our earnest efforts at engagement—offering leaflets or putting on short "guerilla theatre" sketches—were most often politely ignored. It was very frustrating!

I was surprised to discover this lack of engagement extended even to my own pastor, John Meyer, and my great uncle, Arthur Kuehnert. While not agreeing on much related to Vietnam, Pastor Meyer was the senior pastor at our church, and he had listened to and talked with me for numerous hours about the war and the draft. He had been very supportive of our Walther League activities related to world hunger awareness. I knew that he was very active in the district and was seeking election to the board overseeing district affairs. I had naively hoped Pastor Meyer would help us reach other delegates by being friendly and visible around our booth, at least joining in some discussions of the war and racism. Instead, he diligently avoided our booth and, when he and I met at random over the course of the two days of convention, he averted his eyes and, conveniently, was deeply engaged in discussion.

Great Uncle Arthur and his wife, Liode, were as surprised to see me as I was to see them Monday morning, the first day of the convention. Arthur was in his mid-eighties and had retired from his ministry at a north St. Louis church at least 15 years earlier after having served there as pastor for more than 30 years. Throughout his long career in the church, he had also served for decades as chairman of the Mission Board and so was regarded with great respect and affection, particularly in this, his "home" district.

Arthur and Liode attended worship services and a handful of business sessions over the course of the convention, but did not have any official roles. After initially greeting me on Monday morning at our booth, catching up on the doings of our extended family and congratulating me on my position as a staffer with the Walther League, they looked over and took a few copies of our materials, including my "Here I Stand" statement of draft resistance. Then, they left our booth without asking about or making any acknowledgement of my planned draft resistance; they never returned for further conversations. Since we were not particularly close, and my experience of others at the convention was very similar in terms of lack of direct engagement with me, I did not make anything much of our lack of interaction. I would come to greatly regret this much, much later, when I discovered that I was not the first Kuehnert family member to publicly protest the draft during an unpopular war: Great Uncle Arthur's brother, Paul, had resisted the draft during World War I. It strikes me now that when Arthur and Liode walked away from me in 1970, they were likely reacting, in part, to memories of 1917 and the anti-German hysteria (up to and including lynchings) that spread across Missouri and the rest of the country after the

United States entered the war. *That* Paul's protest must have put him—and them and the rest of the extended Kuehnert family—in great jeopardy.

But that Monday morning, I was completely ignorant of my family history of conscientious objection to conscription. Instead, I was thinking about how to get the church's full attention turned to Vietnam the next day when I would turn 18 and, if all went according to my plans, commit a felony.

Shortly after 9 a.m., President Scherer was reporting on the finances of the Missouri District as the convention moved into its closing business session. He looked up with a start—and then with undisguised fury—as we pushed through the rear doors of the gymnasium and marched straight down the center aisle toward the stage with our voices raised in song.

Finally, it was my eighteenth birthday! I was determined that this day was going to be different. Today we were done with talking, being polite, and sitting on the sidelines at our booth. We wanted action.

I never thought they would let us on the stage, let alone leave the microphone on at the podium. So, I had not planned anything to say—just marching, clapping and singing. But now, as we walked up the short flight of stairs to the stage and stopped singing, President Scherer sat down on an empty chair to the side of the stage, glaring at me, but leaving the podium wide open. I moved toward it while the others stood in a line across the front of the stage. All eyes were on me now as silence filled the auditorium.

Feeling a bit woozy, I tapped the microphone, then grabbed the smooth sides of the podium for support and began to speak, my voice cracking with emotion.

"My name is Paul Kuehnert, and I am a member of Concordia Maplewood. I turned 18 today and, so, am required to report to my draft board and register. I am here to tell you that I'm not going to do that, not today. Not tomorrow. Not any day. I will not—no, no—I *cannot* register for the draft. This is because my conscience tells me *I must not*.

"I must, instead, break the law because the law exists only to support the war in Vietnam. And that war, the war in Vietnam, is wrong, morally wrong. It is not a just war. The endless bombing. The invasion of Cambodia just last month. The burning of villages and murder of villagers. The deaths of tens of thousands of soldiers, ours and theirs, and all for what? Nothing, nothing justifies this death and destruction.

"You are my church, and we are all one in the body and blood of our Savior, Jesus Christ. I learned coming up in this church, from a very young age, that I must examine my heart and my conscience and then, follow my conscience, in all matters, great and small. This is the biggest thing, the biggest decision I have ever had to make, and I have made it as you, my church, taught me.

"I know you all may not agree with my stance. But I hope you can agree that I must follow my conscience in these difficult, trying times.

"Please join me, join *us*, in doing what you can to stop the war and stop the draft. We cannot have business as usual as long as this war rages on. PEACE NOW!" I paused and looked across the auditorium. The room of men stared at me from their seats, many with their lips sealed tight in stiff grimaces. Others were shaking their heads "no" and whispering to their neighbors.

I figured I had pushed the situation about as far as I dared, and so I stepped away from the podium and lifted my arms up in a gesture President Nixon had appropriated from the peace movement, forming peace signs with both my hands, pumping them up and down in rhythm with the chant our group had taken up: "PEACE NOW! STOP THE DRAFT! PEACE NOW!" I led our group off the stage, back down the center aisle, and out the rear doors into the sunshine, where we all collapsed into each other's arms in a series of group hugs.

As we laughed and talked, I worked my way from person to person, thanking them for joining me on stage and being a part of my draft resistance action. I went to Dennis and Jane last. I found myself physically shaking as I hugged them, the pent-up anxiety washing out of me. They held me tight. Dennis whispered into my ear, "Welcome to the resistance, brother!"

* * *

The next few days were slow and dull, as my mood sunk into the soupy humidity of the St. Louis summer. My birthday had been on a Wednesday and the following Saturday, my parents and brothers left early in the morning for the traditional family camping trip at Logger's Lake in Missouri's Ozarks. I got up early to see them off. My brothers had grunted at me, got in the car and slumped down in the back seat, hoping to get back to sleep as soon as possible. My mother hugged and kissed me, telling me to be careful, that they would call from the store in town and check in on me in the middle of the week. Tears began flowing when Daddy honked the horn impatiently, shouting out the car window: "Come on, Eunice, let's get going! Times a-wasting!" She turned and walked out to the car, got in the front seat, turned and waved, her face wet and red, as Daddy pulled out of the driveway.

I took off my glasses, wiped my eyes, put my glasses back on and waved back, watching as they took off in the shiny white Ford Galaxy 500 pulling the pop-up camper with the silver aluminum canoe tied on top of it. The car and trailer seemed to be moving in slow motion as I watched it move away up the hill. I was thinking I would probably see my parents next when they bailed me out of jail, since I was convinced I would be arrested sometime in the next week.

"Why don't you shut that door and keep the air conditioning inside the house?" Susie said sharply from the living room behind me. I had not heard her come down the stairs. I shut the door and turned around to face her as I wiped more tears off my face.

"What are you going to do now? Mope around the house like you've been doing all week since your birthday and all your friends left? Jesus,

Paul, is this what it's gonna be like with you until the stupid FBI comes by and hauls you off to jail? Poor little Paulie, you feel so sorry for yourself. "

"What the—? Oh, fuck you, Susie! You don't know, you don't get it. Oh, fuck you!" I stormed past her, ran up the stairs to my room, slammed the door and threw myself into bed, sobbing. The stress and strain of the past week—really, the past year as I had worked my way toward my decision to resist the draft—flowed out of me. I cried and shook for I don't know how long, pushing my face into my pillows to quiet my cries until I fell asleep.

I awoke a few hours later, my face crusty with dried tears and snot. I made my way to the bathroom and washed my face with cold water, avoiding looking at myself in the mirror. Hungry, I made my way down to the kitchen and popped some bread into the toaster. The house was silent.

Susie was at work. She had left a note on the counter with one word: "Sorry."

I smeared peanut butter and jelly on my toast, poured a glass of milk, and sat down at the counter. Halfway through my sandwich, I decided that the antidote to moping.around the house would forward motion—specifically, the forward motion of a Greyhound bus.

I called my friend, Louisa Johnson, in Chillicothe, Illinois. Louisa and I had developed a relationship when I was in Peoria with the Youth and World Crisis team. She was going to Antioch College now, but would be home for another week before her term started, she said, and would be happy to see me. I told her I would catch the next bus and call her from the bus station with my arrival time.

I rushed upstairs and threw some clothes and books into a suitcase. On my way out of the house, I scrawled a note on the back of Susie's: "Off to Peoria to see Louisa, who will cure me of the moping. I hate it when you are right. Back???"

* * *

111

After spending most of the next week with Louisa in Chillicothe, I came home for a couple of days, then left on the Greyhound again, this time to travel across Missouri to Kansas City and meet up with a group of seven Walther League staffers. We were to meet up at Dan Gilbert's house to drive together to Oakland, California, where the whole Walther League youth staff would gather for about three weeks of orientation and training. After completing the training, we would drive back east together to Rosebud, South Dakota, where the Walther League was holding its biennial convention on a campground owned and operated by the Rosebud Sioux. After the convention, I would return to Oakland and begin my tenure as the regional youth staffer for the western United States.

Since I was not anticipating being back home until at least Christmas, I stuffed pretty much every bit of clothing I owned, along with my favorite books and records, in one large suitcase. I had a backpack with a couple of changes of clothes, toiletries, notebooks and the books I was currently reading—as well as my sleeping bag—to complete my travel kit. Since my parents and brothers were still away, Susie took me and all my belongings to the bus station.

As we exited the expressway downtown and neared the station, she reached over and turned up the radio volume.

"Don't look back, but I think we're being followed!" she said in a voice I could barely hear over the music.

"What!? What!?" I said with a start, turning around to look out the back window.

"No, no, seriously, don't!" she said, and then broke into laughter. "I got you! I got you! You are SO, so paranoid, Paul!"

"You! What! I mean, Jesus, why did you do that! Draft resistance is a fuckin' crime and the Feds are likely on to me, you know. It's not paranoid, it's being real!"

"Maybe, maybe. But lighten up or you are going to be a real pain in the ass to everyone you know and are with. Hopefully you weren't obsessed like this when you were with Louisa. You are never going to have a decent girlfriend—"

"Oh. Shut. Up." I stared silently out the side window as she wove her way through the midday traffic to the bus station on the northern edge of downtown. Susie pulled into a parking space. I got out of the car without a word and went off to get a luggage cart. When I got back to the car with the cart, she was standing by the open trunk.

"Don't be mad, Bodie! Really, I know it's scary, but they are in your head when you are like this. You said you were doing this so that you could be free, be your own man. Don't let worry and watching out for them become, well, like some kind of jail or something."

I pulled the heavy suitcase out of the trunk, put it on the cart and then stacked the sleeping bag and backpack on top. I slammed the trunk lid down, turned and faced my sister.

"Maybe you have a point. I mean, well, I know ... It's just hard, like, not knowing what is going to happen." The cart started rolling away from us, and I grabbed its handle. I felt like this was some kind of important moment with my sister, that it was marking a new chapter somehow for both of us since I was leaving home, maybe for good. We had been through a lot together—on picket lines, in jail, in court—and I knew she was my biggest supporter. But I felt weird and unable to put my feelings into words. "Well, you should get outta here before you melt in this heat. I can get this in the station. Tell Mom and Daddy and the boys I got off and I'll call you guys when I get out to Oakland or something, like on Sunday, I think."

I had both hands on the luggage cart and was tensing up to push off when Susie reached over and pulled me into a hug. I steadied the cart with one hand and hugged her back with one arm.

"Ok, Bodie. Be careful. And have fun! I wish I was going to California!"

I smiled, said "OK, bye," and threw my weight into the heavy cart and got it rolling toward the station. Once in the station I glanced back and saw our car turning out of the parking lot and onto Broadway. I swallowed the lump that had risen in my throat and steered my baggage over to the ticket counter.

* * *

Frieda and I were the only ones awake as the huge Pontiac station wagon rumbled along Interstate 80 in the high desert a few hundred miles east of Reno. From my angle in the front seat I could see that she had eased the big car up over 80 miles per hour. I glanced back at the occupants of the two back seats. In the reflected light from cars and trucks passing on the other side of the interstate, it seemed like no one was stirring. We were particularly concerned about Dan, the car's owner, who had given us all very strict instructions that we were not to drive faster than 65. He said it was because of his insurance, but nobody believed him. The first day out, from Kansas City to Estes Park, where we stopped overnight at Dean and Glady Kell's place, everyone cooperated. Since then, the artificially imposed speed limit that was at least five miles lower than the posted limit had been a growing point of friction. Chuck and Wayne, who knew Dan the best because they all went to school together at Concordia Teachers' College in Seward, Nebraska, had argued with him almost all day while Frieda, Betsy, and I just kept quiet.

"Is he out?" Frieda whispered.

"As near as I can tell," I replied. "He's way in the back with Chuck."

"OK, good. Well, it'd be a shame to waste time when it's flat and there is really no traffic. Plus I think out here, just like in west Texas, people go as fast as they want."

Illustrating her point, a semi passed us. Frieda pressed the accelerator a little more to fall in behind the truck, and it looked like she was doing something like 90. "OK, well I feel comfortable with this and it should make up some time from earlier in the day. Now, your job is to keep me awake while not waking up the others. What do you want to talk about? You seem more quiet than usual, Paul."

I took a deep breath. Where to begin? Frieda turned and looked at me, smiling slightly. She took one hand off the wheel, grabbed one of mine, squeezed it, and held it for a minute.

"Just start wherever," she said. "You and Dan told us all about the Missouri District Convention and stuff, but that seemed like more, well, like a report. How are you doing now, what, three weeks into being a resister?"

"I don't know. I mean, kind of messed up, if you really want to know.
"

"Yeah, well, I can kind of imagine."

"Like, for one thing, I am just thinking about this all the time. About being a resister, about being out there, you know, just seeing the Feds everywhere and nowhere, worried. God, it seems like it is all I can think about and talk about." I went on to tell her about a conversation I had with Louisa's mother the week before. "Her Mom was trying to talk to me and said something like 'so, what's next for you?' and I said something stupid like, 'jail I guess.' I then went on and on about a book I was reading called Conscientious Objectors in Prison." Finally, I told Frieda, "When I paused long enough for Louisa's mom to get a word in edgewise she said something like 'I see, but I was really asking about your job. Louisa says you have a cool job and you're not going to college.' And I was, like, 'oh, yeah, that.'" Even while I was relaying this to Frieda, I could feel my face flushing. I felt so embarrassed remembering how embarrassed I had been! Fortunately, she was looking at the road, and, of course, the only light in the car was from the dashboard.

In the nearly two years I had known Frieda, she always had a knack for knowing exactly how to listen and what to say, when; this was one of those times. Over the next hour, she listened carefully as I shared all the worries and concerns that had been animating every one of my waking moments since my birthday. I told her I was deeply worried that I already was becoming isolated and self-centered. Many of my friends who were turning 18 said things to me like, "You are so brave, I could never do what you are doing." This simultaneously put me on a pedestal and kept them from sharing their own struggles about deciding to register for the draft with me. I was worried that my friends assumed I would judge anyone who did not make the same choice about the draft that I did.

On top of those more personal worries, I went on to tell Frieda that I was also concerned that the political impact I hoped for from the resistance movement was illusory. I pointed out what seemed to be the ineffectiveness of the huge antiwar marches of the prior fall in stopping the escalation of the war in subsequent months, especially the massive bombing campaign being waged against North Vietnam and the invasion of Cambodia. I talked about my disappointment with the response we received at the Missouri District convention. If anything, I told her, it seemed like framing my draft resistance as an act of conscience aligned with Lutheran tradition and doctrine just seemed to make church leaders angry, not introspective.

I can't remember everything Frieda said to me as we raced through the night. I know that she spoke about her own experiences, both in the church and in the broader movement. She shared her sense that what we were doing did make a difference. She saw the impact on individuals she worked with over the past two years, including me. Holding on to this belief was hard, she said, and required faith. But not blind faith, faith that was tested in the reality of our experiences.

As she spoke, I could feel the warmth and caring behind her words. I felt understood and, yet, challenged somehow, to think more deeply, to feel more fully. I sat next to her in the front seat and watched the white lane markings steadily flow through the headlight beams in a steady rhythm. I absorbed the quiet thunk of the tires as they sped across the adjoining sections of pavement.

The next thing I knew, I was jerking straight up in the seat with a start and a sudden intake of breath. Frieda looked over at me.

"It's OK if you wanna sleep."

"No, no, jeez, I'm sorry. I said I would keep you company. I must have, well, how long was I out?"

"Oh, just maybe 10 minutes or so. Really, I am OK. "

"But, no, thanks, I mean, really. I was listening to you and what you were saying makes so much sense. You lifted a weight off, or something. And then I just got so relaxed, man. I just must have nodded off."

"Well, good. I'm glad about that. Now, what else do you want to talk about? Maybe we can solve all the world's problems or something?"

"We could, but for some reason they just don't seem to listen to us all the time. So, let's change subjects. I think I overheard you saying that Mike was working at the zoo now. What's that like?"

For the next few hours, I learned about the duties of an assistant zoo-keeper at the Houston Zoo. It turned out that Mike had developed a special interest in a pair of nocturnal bears the zoo had obtained and was trying to breed in captivity. Frieda appeared to me to have fully adopted Mike's passion. For the first time in weeks, I thought and talked about a subject totally unrelated to Vietnam and the draft. It was such a relief.

* * *

The rest of the summer and then the early fall flew by as I threw myself into my work as a regional staffer for Walther League. There were a few surprises along the way, though.

First, during our month-long orientation and training period in Oakland, Dan Gilbert decided that he did not want to work for the Walther League after all. This vacancy, combined with Betsy Hess' decision to leave her position on the East Coast later in the summer, left significant gaps in staff coverage for the League in much of the country, including the Midwest. I eagerly volunteered to be reassigned from the West Coast region to the Midwest, resulting in my new "home base" being Chicago. My region would be focused on only three states: Wisconsin, Illinois and Missouri.

My reassignment to the Midwest led to two additional developments. First, my good friend, Joe Warnhoff, decided to join me in Chicago as an unpaid staff volunteer. This meant that I had a trusted partner to do the day-to-day work of planning, organizing, and carrying out Walther League activities in the region. We connected with two progressive pastors in the near western Chicago suburbs of Maywood and Broadview and, after living for a few months in the semi-finished basement of a parishioner, moved into a small, roach-infested apartment above a restaurant in downtown Maywood. In addition to our church-focused, Walther League work, we quickly connected with local peace and justice activists, including the West Suburban Alliance Against War and Racism, and *Peoples' Voice*, a newspaper produced by a collective of local activists who were focused on organizing tenants and workers in a number of nearby factories.

The second development was more disconcerting. My reappearance in the Midwest put me back on the radar of the President of the Missouri District of the church, Pastor Herman Scherer. In September, President Scherer sent a letter to the Walther League on behalf of the Presidium of the Missouri District, demanding that I be dismissed as a staff member of Walther League because of my draft resistance and my leadership of the group that disrupted the Missouri District Convention in June. While this demand was rejected by unanimous vote of the Walther League Council when it met in October, the demand represented an escalation of the church's disapproval of the League and its new direction.

Then, one evening in early November, I received the call from Daddy that I had been anticipating and dreading: He had been contacted that afternoon by the FBI! A pair of agents would be coming to talk with him the following morning at his office. No, he said, they wouldn't tell him what it was about. Just that they had to meet him right away and in person. Mom got on the phone extension, and I went over everything I knew about FBI interviews I felt surprised at how calmly I spoke and how reassuring I was. Before we hung up, I got Daddy to promise that he would call me at the Walther League office the moment the interview was over and he could talk.

When we hung up, I turned to Joe, who was seated at his desk across the cluttered living room of our tiny apartment.

"The fuckin' Feds, man, the fuckin' Feds ..." my voice cracking. I could feel my heart race as I wiped the palms of my hands on my jeans.

"I heard, man, I heard." Joe shook a cigarette out of the pack on his desk, lit it and passed it over to me. "They don't know what it's about, huh?"

"No, didn't tell him. But what else can it be? Shit, shit, shit! I don't need this, man, not now. We just got started here and now it's going to be all fucked up to sideways. Shit!"

"We better call Mark, and Denny, and—"

"No man, no phones," I interrupted him. "You know that. We have to suppose they know where I am and this phone is tapped. In fact, let's get outta here, away from this phone and talk, you know, about what's next."

We grabbed our cigarettes and matches, threw on our coats and headed through the tiny kitchen out the back door, clomped across the rickety wooden porch, and down the flight of stairs to the gangway behind the restaurant. We dodged trash cans and discarded boxes, then made our way out to Chicago Avenue, turning east toward the park that ran along the banks of the Des Plaines River. It was one of my favorite places to walk and think.

We spent the next two hours walking, smoking and talking, trying to identify all the ways this FBI visit could go for my dad, what he might do or say, and the likely impact on me. Joe had a true gift for processing, sorting, and analyzing information, and quickly came up with what he thought were the three most likely scenarios and their implications: 1) my dad was involved in something I didn't know anything about, some kind of criminal activity having to do with his work, and that there were no implications for me; 2) that my mom and dad were somehow involved in resistance activities themselves, maybe through Denny and Jane, and that it might have implications for me, Joe, and others whom we knew in St. Louis; and 3) that it was, indeed, about me and my draft resistance and that, since it was the St. Louis office, it was likely that President Scherer had called the FBI to report me and that they were being systematic with the investigation, contacting my parents first. We concluded that the third option was the most likely, given the timing of Scherer trying to get me fired just a few weeks back. Cold and out of cigarettes, we made our way to the diner we liked. We bought a pack of Marlboros from the cigarette machine and then sat in a booth smoking and drinking coffee for another hour as we hammered out a plan for the next morning.

Although I was emotionally and physically spent when we got back to the apartment around 9:30 p.m., I doubt that I slept a wink that night. By 6:30 the next morning, we were out the door, headed toward my 1962 Plymouth Belvedere. I was lugging a suitcase crammed with all the clean clothes I had, some books, and my journals. I tossed the suitcase into the trunk and got behind the wheel, while Joe slid into the passenger seat. I cranked the car and it surprised me by catching and starting on the first try.

"You are going to have to get your license, man, and quick!" I said as we merged into the early morning traffic on the Eisenhower Expressway to make our way downtown to the Walther League offices. "You can't leave this car too long in the parking lot, you know." Joe grunted and blew smoke out the cracked window.

The plan we had devised was to go to the office and wait for my dad to call. While there, I would write brief letters to everyone I needed to, alerting them that the FBI was officially investigating me for my non-registration. I was not planning on giving them the opportunity to arrest me, though, and was going to immediately go underground. I was not sure exactly how to make that work, but knew that another Walther League staffer, Pauline Redmond, had extensive contacts in the network that helped the Phil and Daniel Berrigan go underground after their conviction for burning draft files. Nobody, not even Joe, knew, but my first step was going to be to take the Greyhound to Detroit and see Pauline. I would go on from there to wherever. Joe was going to spend the morning talking to everyone he could in the office to borrow money from them for me. We would meet up after the call and debrief, then he would give me whatever cash he had, and I would get on the subway. I would not tell Joe or anyone else at the League offices where I was going, so that no one had to lie to the FBI when they, inevitably, came calling.

We were the first ones in the parking lot behind the offices at 875 N. Dearborn, but I chose a spot in very back of the lot, under a light. I locked the car carefully after grabbing my luggage, then gave the keys to Joe. He unlocked the back door of the office building and pocketed the keys. We made our way to the second floor, started some coffee, and made ourselves at home. We had lived, off and on, in the office for the first month or so we were in Chicago that summer, stretching out in our sleeping bags in the storage room in the basement, so everything about the early morning in the quiet building was comforting and familiar. I busied myself with my letters. Joe talked to colleagues as they came in, one by one or in small groups. It was better for all of them, I thought, to have minimal conversations with me—again, thinking ahead to what I imagined were going to be extensive FBI interviews as the Feds began to search for me, as, what? A suspect. A fugitive!

I chain-smoked and drank cup after cup of coffee. My pulse pounded and my head throbbed as I watched the clock crawl through the early morning: 8:30, Daddy was at work; 8:35, had they come first thing? 8:38, 8:42, 8:46. I distracted myself by writing a long-ish letter to Louisa, even though we had not been in touch since late August. 9:17, 9:21. I wrote letters to Ann and then Denny and Jane. 9:37, 9:40. I distracted myself again by writing to Frieda. Then, sensing the call must come soon, I wrote to Mom and Daddy. Just as I was finishing the letter, Lyndy stuck her head in the door.

"Paul. Your Dad is on 9643." I looked over at the black phone and saw that the middle light was flashing. I thanked Lyndy and she shut the door. I took a deep breath.

"Hello?"

"Hey, Paulo, it's your Dad. Look, this is long distance on the company phone, and I have to be quick, especially since they are not too happy with me here this morning."

"What? I mean, why? Why are they—"

"Ha, well, you know, it's not every day that the FBI shows up here at S & P and talks to one of their engineers, ha-ha!" Daddy didn't sound like himself. He was, well, so happy or excited or something.

"Daddy, what is going on? Are they still there? Do you need to hang up or?"

"No, no. Look, they left. But, you know, Mr. Shem is sitting here, just next to Bob's desk, so I have to make this quick. Turns out it was kind of silly. And not about you, well not really. They wanted to know if I was a supporter of the Black Panther Party! Ha! My car, they told me, was parked outside the Auditorium there on Madison a couple of Sundays back, when Huey P. Newton was holding a big rally in Chicago there."

I gulped. Joe and I had gone to that rally with a bunch of kids from our churches. It was part of a 'live-in" educational experience that we had organized. I remembered that the Plymouth was registered in my Dad's name and had Missouri plates. The FBI must have had the rally under surveillance and noted any out of state license plates.

"But, Dad, why—"

"I know, I know. It makes no sense. But they wanted to know if I liked Huey and if I was giving them money. I told them it was none of their business!"

"What?"

"That's right! I told them that whether I went to the Huey P. Newton rally was not their business. That this is still a free country and we have this thing called a Constitution. So, that was it. I think they were surprised, especially since they were doing it right out here in the middle of the office, didn't even ask to talk to me privately. I think they just want to intimidate people or something, but I am not standing for that!"

I couldn't believe what I was hearing. My daddy, who had argued endlessly with me and with Susie about the foolishness of the Black Panthers and other Black militants, somehow was defending their—and his—constitutional rights to the FBI, in front of his whole office!

"Anyway, I got to go, Paul, and talk to Mr. Shem, you know. Anyway, everything is fine."

"But, Dad, did they ask about—"

"No, your name did not come up and I didn't bring it up. Nothing, nothing on that."

"I, er, I mean. OK, Daddy, well, I will maybe call you and Mom tonight?"

"Yep, OK, do that. Yeah, well look, really, it's all OK and it's gonna be OK. Bye now."

I kept holding the phone next to my ear after he hung up until rapid beeping and "your call cannot be completed as dialed" brought me back to reality. I couldn't believe it! I wasn't going to have to become a fugitive—at least not that morning.

I took off my glasses, rubbed my eyes and stared out into the parking lot for a while, not really looking at anything. My racing heart felt like it was returning to normal. I felt so relieved—and yet, a little foolish, too. I had gotten Joe and all my friends worked up about what I thought would be my imminent arrest—and nothing. I mean, not nothing exactly, because my father was being harassed for me taking a bunch of white kids to see Huey Newton! "Figures, the stupid fucks!" I thought to myself and shook my head. Here they were, the esteemed Federal Bureau of Investigation, harassing a white, suburban electrical engineer for being a Black Panther supporter[3], while said engineer's son had committed a felony—and they didn't seem to know it! "What fools!" I thought, chuckling. I put my glasses back on, grabbed my pile of letters and ripped them into shreds, then threw them into the waste can, and went off to find Joe and share the bizarre-but-good news.

---

3. We would only learn about the full extent of the FBI's massive COINTELPRO or counter-intelligence program directed against a wide array of civil rights, antiwar and other dissidents, that had been set up in 1956 by FBI Director J. Edgar Hoover. Hoover especially despised the Black Panthers. See The Burglary by Betty Medsger, 2014.

LUTHERAN WITNESS REPORTER   July 27, 1969

Two Americans Walk on Moon

July 20, In the Year of Our Lord 1969

Viewpoint

Teen-Ager's Reaction To Denver

By PAUL KUEHNERT
Walther League Representative

I CAME to Denver naively thinking that my Walther League brothers and sisters and I could radically change the priorities of the Missouri Synod from property to people — especially to the have-nots. I left Denver realizing that our church would not make this about-face. At the same time I left Denver firmly convinced that this change of priorities must come now, or the Synod will be a thing of the past.

However, many things impressed me at the convention in many different ways. I was impressed by the ignorance of certain committeemen and chairmen who listened to t' prophetic cries of blacks and young whites and yet did not hear. I was deeply struck by the brotherhood, the fellowship, among the Christians concelebrating the Holy Eucharist. I was disgusted by the politics of some.

The hours spent on trivial resolutions and amendments nauseated me. I was strongly affected by the beauty, power, and courage of the Black Clergy and Black Youth Unlimited.

I was sickened by the hours of endless debate on ALC fellowship when it seems to me that Christ settled that question 2,000 years ago. I was angered by the fact that the official youth delegates appointed by the Districts were not allowed to speak on the floor at all times.

The fact that Synod spent approximately $500,000 for this convention is abhorrent to me. All of these experiences and many others have given me this image of the Synod: It is a group of human beings in which the majority are apathetic and self-centered, continually twisting the words and actions of Christ to please themselves.

SOME OF YOU readers may be extremely angry with me for criticizing our institution in this manner while not proposing any alternative actions. Here is my answer.

First, we must repent and ask forgiveness from God and our brothers for our apathetic and repressive actions in the past.

Next, if we are sincere in our repentance, our priorities will change abruptly — Synod's money will go to bettering the human condition, not to building new seminary chapels.

White people of the Synod must be made aware of their racism, past and present, subtle and blatant, and they must change completely in both attitudes and actions. Both money and spiritual support must be given to the efforts of our black and brown brothers to better their community.

Listen to the words of Isaiah: "Bring no more vain oblations, . . . the calling of assemblies is iniquity, even the solemn meeting. Your new moons and your appointed feasts My soul hateth; they are a trouble unto Me; I am weary to bear them. I will hide my eyes from you . . . I will not hear: your hands are full of blood. Wash yourselves . . . put away the evil of your doings from before Mine eyes; cease to do evil, learn to do well, seek judgment, relieve the oppressed . . ." (Isaiah 1:13-17)

Come on, church, "the time to hesitate is through." We've talked too much. The ship of Synod is sinking fast — I feel we have less than 2 years to pump drastically, or it's sunk. And if the orders don't come SOON to man the pumps and steer in the other direction — the people's direction, which is Christ's direction — and if we don't start acting now, I think a goodly number of us will abandon ship, swim to land, and build a new one.

Paul Kuehnert, a Walther League representative to the Denver convention, is a member of Concordia Lutheran Church, Maplewood, Mo., and a senior at Webster Groves High School.

An opinion piece the author was invited to write for the *Lutheran Witness Reporter in July, 1969.*

Walther League staff, May, 1970, Rosebud, S.D. Sitting in tree from left: Wayne Werning, Pat Krause, Chuck Steinbach, Deb Sweet, Dan Gilbert, Sue Laporte. Front, standing,: Mark Hellman, the author, & Betsy Hess.

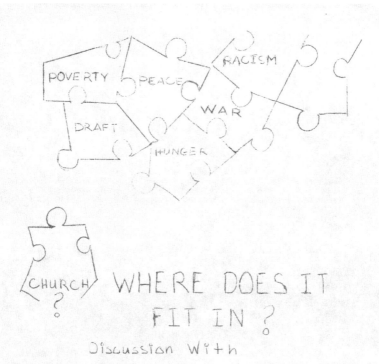

Flier distributed by the coalition of Black Youth Unlimited, the Draft Resistance Action Group, and the St. Louis Hunger Team at the convention of the Missouri District of the Lutheran Church-Missouri Synod, June 14-17, 1970.

"HERE I STAND ....

Brothers and Sisters in Christ,

Because I am one with all of you in the body of Jesus Christ and also in the fellowship of the Lutheran Church-Missouri Synod, I would like to share with you a decision I have made. This decision will drastically affect my life in the near future. On Wednesday, June 17, 1970, I will become 18 years old; and according to the law of the land, I am required to register for the draft within five days of that date. I am a conscientious objector to the draft, however, and will therefore refuse to register.

I do this, believing that as a Christian I must live my life in love and oneness with my brothers and sisters of the human family. Thus I feel that I cannot cooperate with institutions that make possible the killing of human beings and deal with people in an unjust manner. I believe that the draft is one such institution; for it makes warmaking possible by supplying the army with young men to kill and, perhaps, be killed.

I cannot willfully cooperate with the illegitimate exercise of authority, be it governmental or otherwise, or with any other attempt to coerce me into supporting death, hatred, and destruction. I believe that as a Christian I must try to seek, speak, and live the truth, as exemplified by the life of Jesus Christ. I believe that I must commit myself to a life of love, hope, and freedom from fear.

I ask from you, my spiritual community, a response. Together we must bring our powers of love to bear on these times of war, human misery, and injustice. I not only seek your support for my stand as a conscientious objector to the draft but also ask you to search your own lives for your personal response to these times of crisis.

> Paul Kuehnert
> Concordia Lutheran Church
> Maplewood, Missouri

Supported by a convention coalition:
  Draft Resistance Action Group (D.R.A.G.)
  Black Youth Unlimited (B.Y.U.)
  St. Louis Hunger Team (S.L.H.T.)

I CAN DO NO OTHER."
MARTIN LUTHER

The author's statement on his non-registration for the draft, that was distributed by the coalition of Black Youth Unlimited, the Draft Resistance Action Group, and the St. Louis Hunger Team at the convention of the Missouri District of the Lutheran Church-Missouri Synod, June 14-17, 1970.

Flier distributed by the coalition of Black Youth Unlimited, the Draft Resistance Action Group, and the St. Louis Hunger Team at the convention of the Missouri District of the Lutheran Church-Missouri Synod, June 14-17, 1970. We brought the celebration inside and disrupted the District's business meeting.

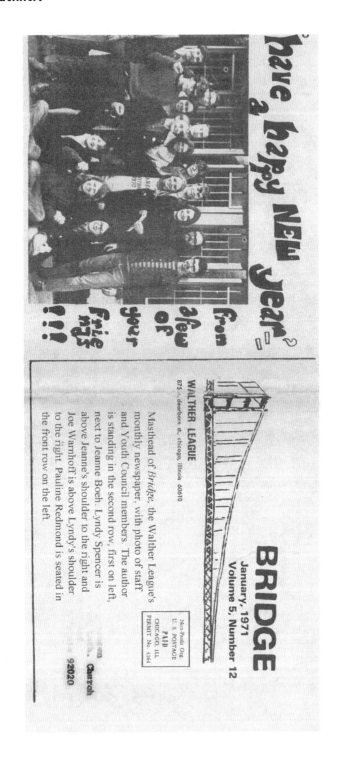

have a happy NEW year from a few of your friends!!!

BRIDGE

January, 1971
Volume 5, Number 12

WALTHER LEAGUE

875½, dearborn st., chicago, Illinois 60610

Non-Profit Org.
U. S. POSTAGE
PAID
CHICAGO, ILL.
PERMIT No. 4164

Masthead of *Bridge*, the Walther League's
monthly newspaper, with photo of staff
and Youth Council members. The author
is standing in the second row, first on left,
next to Jeanne Boeh. Lyndy Spencer is
above Jeanne's shoulder to the right and
Joe Warnhoff is above Lyndy's shoulder
to the right. Pauline Redmond is seated in
the front row on the left.

Front cover of <u>Check Out the Odds</u>, a 70+ page booklet advocating
draft resistance by non-registration that the author contributed to,
published in spring 1971 and sold for 10 cents.

SELECTIVE SERVICE SYSTEM
REGISTRATION CERTIFICATE

0002

STATE NO.	L.B NO	DATE	DUPL	CURR	DELI
11	42	X			

DATE	OF	MAILING
JAN	14	1972

KUEHNERT, PAUL LAWRENCE

308 N PINE AVE.

CHICAGO, IL.   60644

REGISTRANT'S NAME

AND

MAILING ADDRESS

FOLD   FOLD

SELECTIVE SERVICE SYSTEM
NOTICE OF CLASSIFICATION

STATE NO.	LOCAL BOA TO NO.	LOCAL BOARD NO.	AN X INDICATES THAT THIS IS THE		X INDICATES YOU HAVE EXTENDED LIABILITY
11	42		X		
ISSUING THIS FORM	OF RECORD	ORIGINAL	DUPLICATE	CHANGE	DELETION

DATE	OF	BIRTH	RANDOM SEQ. NUMBER
JUN	17	1952	193
			(IF AVAILABLE)

KUEHNERT, PAUL LAWRENCE

308 N PINE AVE

CHICAGO, IL   60644

FOLD   FOL

The author's draft card received after registering in December, 1971 and being classified 1-A

132

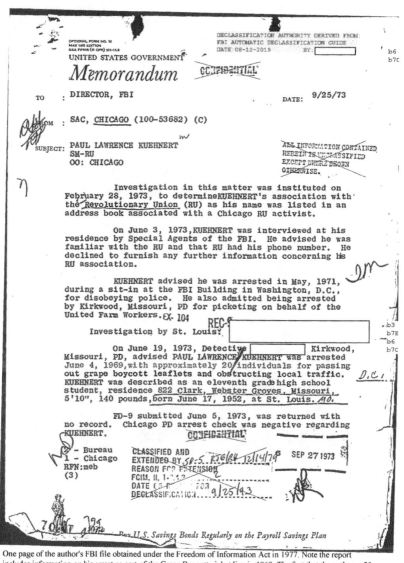

One page of the author's FBI file obtained under the Freedom of Information Act in 1977. Note the report includes information on his arrest as part of the Grape Boycott picket line in 1969. The fact that the author, a 20 year old, White, Midwestern activist, had an FBI file of more 25 pages that was heavily redacted when released in 1977, is an indicator the breadth of the FBI's domestic surveillance of constitutionally protected dissent in the era.

Swords into Ploughshares sculpture by Rev. Josef Mensing, given to the author on his 18th birthday.
Photo credit: Evan Kuehnert.

CHAPTER 6:
MAYDAY! MAYDAY! MAY 1, 1971

We barreled down the Dan Ryan Expressway that Friday morning as Joe fiddled with the radio's tuner. Flipping between AM and FM stations, he finally landed on WSDM and Neil Young's tenor blasted his memorial to the murdered Kent State students from the Plymouth's cheap speakers. Lyndy, a member of the Walther League headquarters staff who we picked up on the north side of Chicago early that morning, was sitting in the middle of the back seat, joined in on the final verse, "...Tin soldiers and Nixon comin', we're finally on our own, this summer I hear the drummin', four dead in Ohio, four dead in Ohio..." It seemed an appropriate tune to start our road trip to Washington, D.C. to join what we hoped would be a week of massive antiwar protests and nonviolent civil disobedience: May Day 1971.

As I drove out of Chicago that morning, I was fully charged with the same energy to do all I could to stop the war that I had begun tapping three years prior when I learned of Vic's death in Vietnam. While feeling hopeful about the potential for protests and nonviolent actions to help stop the war, I had been having growing doubts about the impact any antiwar actions were having on the Nixon administration. After all, they had invaded Cambodia and expanded the vicious air bombing campaign to Laos in the last year, seemingly without any regard to protests or public opinion.

These mixed feelings had drawn me to the May Day 1971 protest when my friend Pauline Redmond told me about what was being planned. Pauline had been a part of a Maryland collective farm loosely affiliated with the Catholic Worker and draft resistance movements before she moved to Detroit to work for Walther League. May Day had been conceived and planned by the nonviolent direct-action wing of the antiwar movement as a strategy to stop business as usual in Washington, D.C. We would use coordinated, nonviolent actions—such as forming human chains across highway on-ramps or having large groups of protesters sitting down and blocking major intersections—-snarling traffic at key points throughout the District. The resulting mass arrests would fill the area jails and clog the courts. Further, it was hoped that government employees would strike—-or, failing that, at least stay home due to the huge traffic jams. Thus, we believed, we could shut down large portions of the U.S. government and disrupt the war effort.

We were driving to Washington by way of Detroit that morning so we could pick up Pauline, and her roommate, Bob. It was a bit of a roundabout way to Washington, but we all felt the detour would be worth it in order to have the time together on the road and during the protests. Besides, as Lyndy pointed out, with five drivers, we could just *drive* and still get to D.C. sometime Saturday afternoon.

And drive we did. We got to Pauline and Bob's mid-afternoon on Friday and took a long break to eat and stretch our legs in their neighborhood near downtown Detroit. By 7 p.m., we were on the road again, heading south to Ohio. Music, conversation, and cigarettes fueled our way down through Toledo, then around Cleveland and southeast toward Pittsburgh. With occasional stops for gas, for bathroom breaks, or driver changes, we still made great time as we wound our way through the hills and mountains of southwestern Pennsylvania and northern Maryland through the dark of the night. Bleary-eyed, I pulled into the parking lot of Word of Life Lutheran Church in northwest Washington, D.C. at 6:30 that Saturday. The pastor had opened the church to the protesters as a place to sleep and find respite during the week of demonstrations that lay ahead.

On Sunday morning, we joined a number of impromptu planning meetings and decided to cast our lot with folks from eastern Michigan who were targeting the Washington Circle and its major thoroughfares of 23rd Street, New Hampshire Avenue, K Street, and Pennsylvania Avenue for disruption. I can remember how receiving copies of the *May Day Tactical Manual* made me realize I was going to do much more than walk in a pro-test march and shout slogans.

After nearly a year of being a public non-registrant for the draft, I was putting myself in a situation that had a very high probability of arrest. Not knowing if I was on some sort of list that the FBI might keep of draft resisters, or, failing that, if through the booking process they might screen for proper draft documents, I thought there was a high probability this protest action would have much larger consequences for me. Late that afternoon I made a call to my parents and let them know where I was and what my plans were, including the likelihood of arrest. I didn't mention my fears that an arrest might lead to the discovery that I was a draft resister, but instead, took the tack of minimizing the entire thing, reminding them that I was already a civil disobedience veteran (thanks to grape boycott protest arrest that led to my Saturday afternoon in the Kirkwood, Missouri jail).

After the call, Joe and I walked off our nervous energy, finding our way around the streets of D.C. and checking out the planned areas for our group action, planned for the following morning. After taking a number of wrong turns, we found our way back to Word of Life where we shared sand-wiches and wine with Pauline, Bob, and Lyndy. With the help of the wine, I surrendered to pent-up exhaustion and crawled into my sleeping bag.

Morning arrived with the smell of coffee and whispered greetings among the clusters of sleeping bags scattered around the church basement. After a quick trip to the washroom, I grabbed a steaming cup of coffee and a slightly bruised apple and huddled with Joe and the rest of our small group. After a little anxious chatter, we checked to make sure we each had water and kerchiefs in anticipation of tear gas. At 5:15 or so, we made our way up the stairs and out the side door into the gray morning.

Our group of roughly 15turned right on 20th Street and began walking at a steady pace to cover the five blocks to our assembly point in a parking lot on K Street, a block from the Washington Circle. As we walked, I noticed a handful of other groups of what I assumed to be other May Day protesters walking in the same direction. As we got closer to the Circle, the individual groups began to meld together spontaneously, so that by the time we reached the rendezvous point, our group had swollen to at least 35, joining about 25 others already milling around the parking lot. With a few nervous head nods and "hey, mans," I acknowledged a couple of folks I recognized from the previous afternoon's planning meeting. I lit a cigarette and stood next to Joe and Lyndy, watching Pauline make her way over to a short, bearded guy with blue kerchief knotted around his neck and a megaphone in his hand. They huddled for a minute and then Pauline laughed, turned around, and came walking back toward us.

The man with the megaphone lifted it to his mouth and pushed its button: "OK, people, this is it. It's time for us to step off and get over to the Circle. We are going to shut this fucker down!!"

He turned and walked over to the sidewalk, people bunching up behind and alongside him. He lifted the megaphone again and began a series of rhythmic chants that the crowd soon joined:

One, two, three, four, we don't want your fucking war!
What do we want? Peace! When do we want it? Now!

As we got to the light at K and 21st, we spilled off the sidewalk into the street and moved into the intersection en masse, against the light. Washington Circle was still a block away, but the group slowed in the middle of the intersection, a number of people shaking clenched fists in the air in time with the chant. Traffic began backing up in all directions. I looked around and caught Joe's eye, grinning. "It's working, man, it's working!" I said.

"Damn straight!" said Joe. Horns began beeping individually and then grew into their own chorus, adding to growing excitement. Our leader stopped his chanting and motioned to the crowd to quiet. A faint siren could be heard back in the direction from which we had come. "OK, OK, let's get moving!" he said. "We need to get up there and get on the Circle. If we can to stop the cars, stop this war! Let's get a move on! Go, go, go!" He began jogging down the street, chopping the air with his fist, and shouting "Peace, now! Peace, now!"

We all jogged along and behind him, moving rapidly down the ramp. I heard a growing number of sirens as we approached the ramp, and then began moving down the incline toward the Parkway. Traffic was completely stopped behind us, and as we surged forward, motorists on Pennsylvania Avenue and 22nd Street slowed down to view the spectacle.

A few protesters moved ahead of the crowd and onto the edge of the Circle itself, motioning for cars to slow down and stop. A white Ford station wagon swerved toward a knot of protesters on the grass alongside the Circle, its shouting driver giving us the finger, then turning back into his lane of traffic at the last minute. Lyndy, Joe, and Pauline reached the edge of the Circle and took tentative steps into the near lane. There were now about 15 people in the roadway now, and as I started to follow them, I looked back over my shoulder and saw that K Street itself was completely blocked. I also noticed an advance group of five or six helmeted police officers carrying billy clubs clustered at the corner of K and 22nd streets.

"The cops, the cops!!" I shouted, drowned out by the chorus of "Peace, NOW!" and honking horns. I moved into the Circle, where traffic was now successfully stopped on our side and beginning to slow down and grind to a halt around the entire Circle. More of us surged onto the street, and the cacophony of horns, sirens and chants grew. Our megaphone-armed leader jumped up on the divider and turned back toward the crowd on K Street and in the Circle, seeing the police for the first time.

"OK, people, OK. Move on up, move on up. Let's get some people over the divider and stop it on the other side there. Let's go, let's go, and get this fucker done before the cops come down here!"

I felt I was on autopilot now, trying to read the situation as it unfolded and stay as close to my small group of friends as I could. About half of our larger group was in Washington Circle itself, clustered tightly together at the K Street entry into the Circle and across four lanes of traffic. The other half had noticed what had turned into a phalanx of at least 30 police in full riot gear back at 22nd and K. People began walking into the middle of the circle on the grass, away from the police.

"Hey, come on! Discipline, discipline—-let's get all over here and sit in the road. Sit down! Sit down! Sit down!"

Twenty or so people sat down. Just then, the police began moving in a line down the street, face masks down and clubs tightly grasped. As the line approached, more protesters peeled off and started running alongside the traffic, away from the police and the sitting protesters. Our small group, led by Pauline, ran to the Pennsylvania Avenue entry to the circle and joined a handful of others standing among the stopped cars. While on the other side cars had been stopped in back of the protesters—a group of 25 or so who were now sitting on the pavement—on our side, traffic had snarled in a massive gapers' block with no clear line. We could only stand and walk back and forth among the cars, nervously eyeing our seated comrades as the police approached.

The officer leading the line also had a megaphone: "Disperse! Disperse! This is an illegal assembly and you are breaking the law! Move out of the roadway! Move it! Or you are under arrest!"

At least half our original group was running across the circle now, away from the police. A small group of cops broke off and began giving chase. The others closed in on the group sitting in the roadway, now chanting, "Stop the war! Stop the war! Shut it down and stop the war!"

Our little group moved again, this time to the grass on the far side of Pennsylvania Avenue and 22nd Street and huddled. Joe thought we should cross back over and sit down. I looked at my watch and noticed it was only 6:40 a.m. Traffic was at a complete standstill, and a police bus was now visible in the intersection of K and 22nd. Bob sided with Joe, while Lyndy and Pauline said we should get out while we could and go to another targeted intersection. I was leaning toward the idea of moving on when we saw three cops heading across the divider in the middle of Pennsylvania Avenue and yelling at us that we better get out.

"Let's go, let's go, up 22nd street, come on!" I shouted. We were joined by another small group of stragglers and started making our way up the hill, toward I street. Suddenly, the three cops were behind us, tapping their clubs on the palm of their hands with menacing thwacks.

A beefy, Black cop closed in: "Move it, you fuckers, you fuckin' hippie bastards! Get outta here, get out! You sad fucks, we are going to whip on you something awful if you don't get out and stay the fuck out of our roads."

We reached I street and turned left, going toward the George Washington University. The cops kept up their pace and their patter right behind us, effectively herding us toward the campus. We came up to an intersection that had a gas station on one corner. Someone before us had taken five tires that had been stacked in front and rolled them into the intersection. Traffic was snarled as the motorists worked their way around the obstacles.

"You bastards, you stop right here," the big cop shouted as he simultaneously grabbed me from behind and pushed me out in the street toward one of the tires. "You pick those tires up, you faggot, and the rest of you fucks help him." I walked over and grabbed the tire, set it up and rolled it toward the station. Joe and Bob fetched the others. "You chicks, stack 'em up pretty now, yeah, make it nice. OK, OK, now look you stupid mother-fuckers, you better get off my street. I don't know where you wanna go, but I'll give you a minute before we just run your asses in. And don't let me see you anywhere else, neither, or there is gonna be hell to pay, you got it? Now get out!" With that, he shoved Joe and me in the direction of the campus. We all scurried off down I Street toward 21st Street and the main area of the campus as the cops stopped at the corner, joking and laughing with each other.

"I thought I was done for, man," I said to our group as we got half a block away from the cops. "Christ-on-a-crutch, I mean, when he grabbed me—"

Joe lit a cigarette and passed it over to me. We stopped and stood together a little further down the street, where a crowd of a few hundred protesters was starting to gather in the university yard and around some of the residence halls. There was a buzz of excited conversation as people recounted their morning's exploits.

We found some space on the steps in front of Samson Hall and sat down. Sirens wailed in the background. As the minutes ticked past, additional groups straggled in from all directions; students wandering out from the residence halls joined the crowd as it slowly swelled and began spilling into the street. From time to time, antiwar chants would be started by a small group and then picked up by the crowd.

There was no focused activity, and no one seemed to be taking charge. The five of us were discussing heading back to the church and getting some food and coffee, when cries of alarm rolled through the crowd. By standing on the top steps and looking two blocks away on 21st , we could see that a set of police buses had been pulled up and now blocked off the street. As we watched in disbelief, soldiers in combat fatigues with gas masks on and holding rifles with fixed bayonets filed in front of the buses and lined up in ranks about five deep facing the crowd. Protesters in the front of the crowd half a block away from the soldiers began shouting and shaking their fists:

The people, united, will never be defeated!

The people, united, will never be defeated!

As one, the people came off the steps and sidewalks and surged into the streets, chanting and moving toward the assembled soldiers.

We had joined the spontaneous movement into the street and were probably in the middle of the crowd, a block or so back from the front. Suddenly, there were a series of loud bangs and tear gas canisters rained down in front and on both sides of the crowd. At the same time, the troops stepped off, moving forward.

Chanting was replaced with cries and chaos as the gas enveloped the crowd. I grabbed my kerchief out of my back pocket and held it to my mouth and nose, as I turned, grabbed Lyndy's hand and moved with her back toward the Student Union. Caught up in the now-running crowd, I felt my eyes, mouth, and nose burning as tears flowed freely down my cheeks. I coughed and gagged. Alternately pulling and being pulled by Lyndy, we found ourselves quickly separated from Joe, Pauline, and Bob, and took off down a side street. We followed a group of others who had rushed into a street-level apartment and sputtered our way down the hall to the kitchen in the back. There we took turns bathing our eyes and faces in cold, running water at the kitchen sink, wetting our kerchiefs, and trying not to rub our eyes.

Time stopped as we stood around the sink, gasping and gathering ourselves, waiting for the burning and tears to subside.

"Whose place is this?" I wondered out loud, and nobody seemed to know. A woman with red hair and an even redder face walked back up the hall to the front door and shut it.

"The pigs are all over the street in front," she reported to us as she came quickly back down the hall. "We better get out the back here if we can." She opened the back door and we trooped out, following a sidewalk through a small backyard to a gate next to a garage—-and into an alley.

Distant shouts greeted us, accompanied by an almost continuous wailing of sirens, near and far. The smell of tear gas hung in the air.

We left our companions at the end of the alley, turning left on F. Thanks to Lyndy's unfailing sense of direction, we found our way as quickly as possible back to Word of Life, hurried into the bathroom, and resumed rinsing our eyes with cold water. After about 10 minutes, we dried our faces and went back out into the basement where we had slept the night before, flopped onto our sleeping bags, and waited for our friends to return. As I stared up at the ceiling and took a deep breath, I felt the tension in my neck and shoulders begin to release. Replaying the events of the morning, I realized I had never been so afraid. I shuddered, sought out Lyndy's hand, gave it a soft squeeze, and held on as I drifted off.

"What the FUCK is wrong with you!" Joe's voice startled us and we both sat straight up on the sleeping bag we had fallen asleep on.

"Uh, well, uh, Jesus! You guys are OK?"

"Yeah, yeah, but fuck, man, we were looking all over for you after they shot the gas at us. Where did you go? And then, you didn't meet us like we said, at the rally point, down at K. We were SURE you two got arrested or SOMETHING!"

I looked down at my watch. It was after noon. Lyndy and I had been asleep for about three hours while Joe, Pauline, and Bob were on the streets.

"Oh, shit, man, I am sorry! I totally forgot about that plan we made yesterday," I said, apologetically.

"Yeah, we got swept up by the crowd after the gas, and ended up in some chick's apartment. The cops were all around there and so we just snuck out and found our way back here. God, that was too fuckin' scary."

Pauline and Bob hurried into the basement, carrying a bag of oranges and three cups of coffee. Bob was grinning: "You gotta stop all the shouting of FUCKING FUCKS and SHIT, you dopes! This is the FUCKIN' House of the Lord and the FUCKIN' church ladies are upstairs, passing out coffee and fruit! Watch your FUCKING potty-mouth there, girl," and he grabbed Lyndy into a long hug and gave him an even longer kiss.

We dragged over the others' sleeping bags and flopped down to eat oranges and drink coffee. We spent the rest of the afternoon regaling each other with our adventures after the tear gas, discussing what was going right and wrong with the protest across the city and planning our next move. That night, the basement was about half as full of protesters. We had escaped being arrested that day, but thousands were already in D.C.'s jails, including a dozen or so of our Word of Life comrades. I remember thinking that our plan must be working, and the next day would surely shut the government down completely. So what if it would take thousands more of us to spend a few days in jail?

* * *

Tuesday was another early morning. In our Monday evening discussions, we had reached consensus to join the sit-in that was going to be staged at the Justice Department at noon. May Day organizers had spread the word that more than 7,000 protesters had been arrested Monday, severely straining the capacity of the city's jails. The Tuesday sit-in was going to highlight the role of Nixon's Justice Department in actively suppressing the peace and civil rights movements, as well as continue the effort to grind the federal and city governments to a halt by filling the jails.

Fully expecting to be arrested by the end of the day and jailed for an unknown length of time, I spent some time after breakfast washing up and changing my underwear and socks. Friends who had previously been arrested and spent time in various local jails had advised me to wear jeans, a long-sleeved shirt, and a jacket despite the warm spring weather, as the conditions in the jails were an unknown in terms of cleanliness, temperature, dampness, and so on. I remember staring at myself in the scratched bathroom mirror, wondering if I was really ready for jail—and if my future now would include a lot more time behind bars because of what I was about to do. I pulled on my jean jacket, catching a whiff of yesterday's tear gas, ran my hands through my frizzy, shoulder-length hair, and shook my head. "Fuck it, man!" I whispered to my image and jerked open the bathroom door.

By 8:30 a.m., the 30 or so of us left at Word of Life were ready to get moving. We trooped up the two flights of stairs from the basement to the street and pushed through the metal double doors into the bright morning on 20th Street. We only had about two miles to cover to get to the National Mall in back of the Smithsonian Museum, where we were to assemble before marching the few blocks over to the Justice Department.

We walked briskly in small groups and covered the distance to the Mall in about 45 minutes. As we approached, we could see a few dozen small groups of people milling around in front of the Smithsonian—people who did not appear to be tourists.

"Looks like it's going to be 'small-but-spirited,'" Joe grumbled to me as we stood sizing up the situation.

"It's early yet, man. We got here real early," I countered. "We'll see." We plopped ourselves on the grass and squinted up at the sun. The ground was cool and slightly damp. We propped our heads up on our hands and watched as Lyndy and Bob skipped off holding hands to the other side of the park. Pauline walked around to the groups, talking and laughing. In the distance, along Constitution Avenue, school buses were beginning to pull up and park along the park. I remember wondering where the kids from the buses were, but didn't give it a second thought.

I must have dozed off. Pauline was standing at my feet, nudging them with her boot. "Hey, sleepy head! Hey! Rise and shine!"—a phrase I had heard from my mother throughout my childhood; I had thought she made it up. I sat up, and reached in my jacket for a cigarette, lighting it.

"What, what's going on, Pauline? Where are the others?" I asked.

"It's starting up. Joe and Bob and Lyndy are right up there. Get up and you'll see."

She gave me her hand and helped me up. Sure enough, I could easily find the three others in the crowd ahead. And it had become a crowd, growing in the hour I was napping, from less than 100 people in the park to a crowd that must have been 10 times larger, and growing. As we looked around, people were coming into the Mall in various-sized groups, one large contingent chanting as they entered:

One side's right, one side's wrong!
We're on the side of the Vietcong!
Ho Chi Minh! Madame Binh!
NLF is gonna win!

"Oh, boy! Even the fucking Maoists are here! Lucky us," I grumbled.

"Yeah, yeah, well they have to go with our discipline, and not start anything," Pauline replied.

"Sure, if you say so, Pauline. I hope so. And say, where are all the kids that came on those school buses?" I pointed to the row of yellow that now stretched three-quarters of the way around the Mall—something else that had grown considerably while I slept.

"Those? You are too funny!" Pauline said. "Those are for us!! We snuck up to a few and peeked in—-they're driven by cops and some have bunches of cops just sitting in there. They're assembling just like we are."

"Oh, wow, of course, I guess. Well, this is really going to happen then."

Our eyes met and locked. She reached over and pulled me into a long hug. "It's going to be OK. We are really shutting them down. I don't think they will do anything with you once they have you, man. I think they aren't that organized. They're scrambling and improvising just to do this." She lifted her hands and motioned toward the school buses. She grabbed my hand and held it, leading me over to Bob, Lyndy, and Joe.

At that moment, though, I really didn't want to go along. Instead, I wanted to pull Pauline over to a park bench and tell her how scared I was that my arrest would lead to the FBI getting me for draft resistance and that I would be off to jail for years. We hadn't talked about this, but I really looked up to Pauline. I figured she had been involved in some serious resistance work, maybe even with the last bunch of draft board break-ins that had taken place, resulting in thousands of files destroyed while no one took public responsibility. It was a new tactic, and it required strength and discipline—all of which radiated from Pauline. Surely, I thought, she could help me feel stronger. Instead, I let the moment pass.

For the next hour, we stood and watched the crowd grow as the park become enclosed by a wall of school buses. Close to noon, more organized chanting started from the 'front of the crowd nearest the Smithsonian, and was soon picked up by all, becoming a wall of sound as we moved toward Constitution Avenue and the Justice Department.

The people, united
Will never be defeated!
Peace! Now!
Peace! Now!

We surged into Constitution Avenue, fists and peace signs punching the air in time with the chants, moving toward 9th Street and the Justice Department. As we entered 9th Street with the Justice Department on our left, we could see that the end of the street was blockaded by a line of squad cars and, behind them, a line of school buses that were visibly filled with men. As the demonstrators filled the street from curb to curb and surged forward from Constitution Avenue, cops began filing off the buses and into the street, creating a line of riot-gear clad officers in front of the squad cars.

A group of demonstrators with megaphones scrambled up the steps in front of the entrance to the Justice Department. Others followed with a small portable generator, a set of large speakers, and a microphone. Another group of about 20 men and women formed a security perimeter around the stairway, facing both the street and the doors of the Justice Department. As the technical crew set up the impromptu sound system, a tall, thin, bearded man with a blonde ponytail began to speak using the megaphone: "Brothers and sisters, come on, come on in! Fill up the street here in front of the Nixon Department of Injustice. Spread out, spread out, and go on right up to the police line, right up there so that we have enough room for everyone coming in from across the street. Come on, come on, come on."

We had been toward the front of the march and off to the other side of the street, away from the Justice Department. We worked our way back now, into the middle of the street and directly in front of the main doors and what was becoming the speaker's stage. I looked back toward Constitution and the Mall and saw the last of the marchers coming into what had become a plaza in front of the Justice Department. As the marchers crossed into the demonstraters' space, a line of police in riot gear walked across 9th Street behind them and formed a line, effectively closing the street. The screech of the PA system coming to life brought my attention back to the speaker.

"Sisters and brothers, brothers and sisters, can you hear me? Can you hear me?" the man with the ponytail asked.

A roar went up from the crowd.

"Look, we are here, here in front of the Nixon police, in front of John Mitchell, the Attorney General, to say ENOUGH! Enough of your illegal war! Enough of your invasions, your bombing! Enough of your bogus peace plans—-ENOUGH! My name is Jerry and I am here with other members of the May Day Collective and the Ann Arbor Conference on a People's Peace. Were you a part of our action yesterday?"

The crowd roared back: "YES!"

"Awesome!! Well, more than 10,000 of us hit the streets yesterday and we disrupted the war machine! We stopped the government from its focus on making war yesterday and instead, they had to focus on arresting their people. More than 3000 of us went to jail yesterday, and most are still there! The D.C. jails are full! And now, and today, we are back, back to bring home the message of peace and make clear that war is not without a price. We will not be silent! We will not allow business to continue as usual!"

Chants of *Peace! NOW! Peace! NOW!* over and over stopped his speech for a good minute or two.

"Beautiful! Beautiful!" Jerry continued. "Our spirit is strong, our numbers are strong! Look around you! Look at this street! There are at least 2,000 of us here and we fill the street! Fill the street in front of John Mitchell and his cronies who do nothing to stop the illegal war! Who do nothing to protect our right to protest and instead have ordered the arrest of us by the thousands! Mitchell and his Justice Department are not defending voters' rights and civil rights, but are harassing us, spying on us, looking for every way possible to stop our movements for peace and justice.

"And so we are here today to say 'no' to Mitchel and Nixon! To say 'no' to business as usual! And to say 'no' to the war and to the injustices with the most powerful tool we have: ourselves! We put our bodies on the line to stop Nixon's war in Indochina, and to stop racism and to stop the war on the poor, and on Black America.

"You came here today, my brothers and sisters, to act. We are now going to act—-by sitting down! Sit down! That's right, sit down right there in the middle of 9th street, until John Mitchell resigns for all his crimes and until Congress adopts the People's Peace Treaty."

We looked at each other, shrugged, and sat down in the street. Over the next couple minutes, the crowd found its collective seat. Only a few protesters could be seen edging their way around one of the lines of cops and leaving the demonstration.

Jerry passed the microphone to a Black woman, who gave another short speech punctuated at multiple points by the crowd chanting slogans. A D.C.-based folk group provided a spirited rendition of Phil Ochs' antiwar anthem, "I Ain't Marching Anymore," followed by another speaker. As that speaker was making the case for a United Nations war crimes investigation of Nixon and Henry Kissinger, a Black police officer came out of the doors of the Justice Department, accompanied by four cops in riot gear. The speaker halted mid-sentence as he heard the anxious buzz from the crowd and the security circle around him. He stepped away from the mic and walked toward the cops, conversing for 15 seconds with the officer. The speaker broke off and motioned the cop to the microphone.

"I am Captain Nathaniel David of the Capitol Police. I am here to inform you that you constitute an illegal assembly. You must disperse. You must get up out of the street and move to either end and exit. This is a warning. If you do not disperse in 10 minutes, you will be arrested. You must disperse now."

As he spoke, the crowd began booing, whistling and shouting, *PEACE! NOW!* and drowning out his final words. He turned and spoke again with the May Day Collective leaders who had been speaking, and then walked back into the Justice Department along with his escort. As he walked away, the crowd cheered.

Jerry motioned for silence, and the crowd hushed. "We continue with our program!" he said. "We continue to refuse to move until our demands are met. Stay seated, brothers and sisters, stay seated. We will not disperse. We will fill up the jails of this city until the war is stopped and until the criminals Mitchell, Nixon, and Kissinger are brought to justice."

In a far section of the crowd a new chant began, and soon everyone picked it up:

Nixon and Mitchell

Better start shakin'

Today's pig is

Tomorrow's bacon!

The musicians came back and played and sang. As we sat, we could see activity at either end of the street as the cops changed their formation to accommodate the setup of a few dozen tables and chairs. Buses started and were maneuvered closer to the tables. Good to his word, after 10 minutes, Captain David came out again and walked up to the microphone. "I am Captain Nathaniel David of the Capitol Police," he reminded us. "You have refused my order to disperse. You are receiving no more warnings. You are now under arrest!"

A huge cheer erupted from the crowd.

"Stay seated where you are until an officer comes for you. You are under arrest." Captain David handed the microphone back to Jerry.

"OK, man, you heard what he said," Jerry said. "Stay where you are and we will continue with the entertainment and the educational program. Power to the people!"

It takes a long time to arrest roughly 2000 people, including a sizable minority who refused to cooperate at all and had to be carried off the street, limp, into the buses. I felt I had made my point well enough by being arrested; I didn't feel a need to risk additional charges or, perhaps, provoke an unstable cop into a beat-down by going limp. The police systematically moved from each end of the street toward the center, two cops escorting each individual protester to a table for booking and escorting them onto a bus. Protesters were divided by gender, and any juveniles arrested were taken to a separate area for holding and then transportation to the juvenile authority.

When my turn came, it must have been mid-afternoon, 3 p.m. or a little later. By that point, the protest had turned fairly festive with a great deal of music and—-shortly after the first arrests—-a wedding ceremony. There were only occasional short speeches and chants, with the "tomorrow's bacon" chant gaining more popularity with the crowd.

As the cops closed in on us for the arrests, we all agreed that we would meet back in the church whenever we got out. I was escorted over to a table and looked back to see Joe taken off in another direction. He had decided to tell them right away that he was a juvenile and hoped to avoid being taken to a city jail. The cops stood by me as I was processed, giving my name, birthdate, and parents' home address as my home since it lined up with my only ID, my Missouri driver's license. Giving my parents' address as my own reminded me of the worry in their voices when I had talked with them on the phone Sunday night. I could imagine them watching the national evening news and being anxious about what might be happening to me. I was fingerprinted and then gave my best smirk during the Polaroid® shot taken of me standing between the arresting officers in lieu of an official mug shot. As I was escorted over to the bus, I breathed a sigh of relief that no one had asked for a draft card. I began feeling like I might get through this without being passed over to the FBI for being a draft non-registrant.

The cop sitting in the driver's seat told me to sit down, and I saw that almost all the seats were taken. I sat next to a guy with a scraggly red beard and greasy brown hair; he was wearing a heavy navy pea coat and sweating profusely.

"Hey, man, I'm Paul. Looks like this thing is almost full."

"Yeah, yeah. I'm Bill. I hope they get this rolling and OPEN THESE FUCKIN' WINDOWS YOU PIGS!"

The cop driver looked in our direction and shook his head.

"What is with the coat, man?" I asked. "It's like eighty or something out there."

"These FUCKING PIGS were going to beat us today, I just knew it, so I wore this to protect myself. I had a metal army helmet too, man, but THESE FUCKERS took it away from me, THE FUCKERS STOLE MY SHIT!"

"OK, well that really sucks," I said.

Bill began pounding on the window next to his seat. At this point, I realized that Bill was either on something like speed or mentally unstable. More guys had gotten on the bus, and two cops were conferring with the driver. One told me to move, pointing to an empty seat further back, and then he sat down next to Bill.

"Shut the fuck up and sit still, or the cuffs are going on!!" the cop told Bill, who glared at him, but stopped pounding the glass. The bus engine roared to life and the front doors shut.

The other cop turned and spoke to all of us: "OK. You are done being booked and we are taking you to jail. This is going to be a little bit of a ride, so just relax. We are taking you out to Virginia because the jails here are full—"

A cheer erupted from all of us, and a loud voice shouted: "Stop the war! Shut it down!"

"OK, OK, look, quiet down! Your part is done and we have you now, so just enjoy the ride. It'll be a ways."

The bus lurched forward, falling into a line of buses heading east on Constitution, toward the highway. We had a police escort and so rolled through a series of lights and quickly onto 395, crossing the river and heading into Virginia. A buzz of quiet conversation filled the bus. For many of us, not too far removed from our high school field trip days, the ride felt comfortable and familiar. The only discordant aspects of the scene were the police car escorts with their red lights flashing rhythmically, leading and tailing the bus caravan.

After about an hour, we exited the highway in what was likely Loudoun County. We drove on a winding two-lane highway for another 15minutes before coming into a small town. We wound our way down a couple short blocks, past a stately old courthouse, and turned into the parking lot behind it. Set back a half-block or so from the edge of the parking lot was a modern, brick two-story structure with very few windows, surrounded by a chain-link fence topped with five rows of barbed wire.

The buses stopped at the edge of the walkway leading to a gate outside the building and Cop Number Two, as I thought of him, stood up again, next to the driver.

"Welcome to the Leesburg jail," he said. "Sheriff Deaver has agreed to hold you all here until we can get you back into D.C. for arraignment hearings. We are putting you in a block of cells with the others on the other buses. You will not be mixed in with the other prisoners and you will not take part in their regular activities. Now, stay put until the deputies come and bring you into the jail."

We watched as the buses in front of us were unloaded in turn by a group of about 10 deputies with their billy clubs at the ready, escorting each group up the walk and into the jail building. When it was our turn, Cop Number Two went to the back of the bus, and Cop Number One took Bill off first, walking him to jail by himself. Cop Number Two ordered us to stand and file off the bus, then stand still as a group between the line of deputies waiting on the walk. We were then to hustle down the walk and into the jail building. As we entered, we saw a cordon of deputies blocking our path and motioning us to the right, where we entered a short hallway and were halted. A tall man in a deputy uniform and a crew cut stood in front of us: "You boys are in our jail now and we expect you to live by our rules," he said. "Don't speak unless spoken to. Do what you are told. Then you will be OK. We are holding you for the District of Columbia and your arraignment. That is all we know. We have no other information, so don't ask. Now, there is a drinking fountain on the way into our cell block and you can get a drink. We are working on getting you some food. Now, move along."

We strung out into a single file and moved to the drinking fountain. I took my turn, greedily downing about five gulps of the stale-tasting, coolish water before a deputy told me to move on. I moved on down the hall and, at the entry into the cell block, was grouped with another seven guys and put into an eight-by-ten=foot cell with a sheet metal bunk bed fastened to one wall, a toilet and sink on the other.

"Hey, this is for two men! There are eight of us in here! Wait a minute, officer!"

"Bet you learned to count in that college you go to, huh?" said the deputy, grinning as he swung the door shut and moved to the next cell with another group of eight. "You girls enjoy your stay!"

Early on, the group of 200 or so men in the cellblock joined together in various peace chants, as well as a handful of songs ("All we are saying, is give peace a chance"). As the afternoon dragged into the evening, our collective energy flagged, and the chanting and singing was replaced by the quiet buzz of dozens of conversations.

Over the next several hours, my cellmates and I spent the time getting to know each other and figuring out a routine for managing ourselves in the cramped quarters of the two-man cell. We developed a rotation system so that at any one time we had four guys sitting or lying down on the two skinny bunks and four guys sitting or standing in the various, small open spaces in the cell.

The first time I got a chance to sit on a bunk, I found myself sharing it with the only man in our cell who didn't have long hair and, in fact, looked more like someone from the baseball team in high school. He held out his hand. "I'm Jack. Here from Turkey."

"What? I mean, I'm Paul and live in Chicago. You said Turkey? What, I mean, how—"

"Long story, man. Made a mistake when I graduated high school back home in Ohio and signed up with the Air Force. Lived to regret that when they shipped me over to Turkey a year ago. There it was just boring and we would fly regular patrol missions and stuff. Then the word came down that we were going to the Philippines to fly bombing missions over Vietnam or Cambodia or whatever, so I quit."

My eyes widened. "Wait. They let you quit, just like that?"

"No, no. I just quit, you know. I decided I couldn't be a part of the war machine, you know? I talked to the other guys in my unit and tried to get them to quit too. But, everybody is afraid. Fuck that, I just left, I guess. I was thinking about going to Sweden or Canada or some shit, but this is my country too, you know?"

I was blown away. This guy, Jack, was a deserter. A real resister. And here I was, in the same cell, having the chance to rap with him.

Another guy was sitting on the floor next to us, listening. He said: "Man, you are brave to do that. My name is Phil." He shook Jack's hand and then nodded at me and shook mine for good measure.

"Yeah, Jack," I said, "You are putting yourself out there. What made you do that? I mean, did you change your mind somehow after you joined up? And then how did you decide to join in this action and get put in here with us?" I was excited now, and talking rapidly.

Jack was quiet for few seconds while his eyes searched the space above my head. "I don't know, man, I mean, lots of things. Mainly, the longer I thought about it, the more I knew what we are doing in Vietnam is wrong. Like, I was brought up to be a Christian, and I read stuff about what makes a war just. This is not a just war and so, really, my faith tells me I can't do this anymore. I just can't, not in good conscience. Once I knew that, I mean really knew that, I had to do something: I left. I got some help from antiwar people that run a coffeehouse in Izmir and got through Europe and eventually to New York. This thing, I mean today, I don't know, I was just passing through, you know, hitching my way home to Ohio. This is my first protest and it's pretty cool."

By the time Jack finished, I was smiling widely and nodding. I hadn't felt this quickly connected to another man since I had first connected with Denny Cummins in St. Louis more than 18 months ago. I quickly told him the short version of my draft resistance story and my current work for the Walther League.

Phil had been silent the whole time, but was clearly tracking our conversation, nodding at some points and shaking his head at others. Finally, he spoke up. "Look, guys, I mean I respect you both, you are both really living your convictions and everything. But I think there is another thing you have to think about. This is a vicious government, it's a racist, warmongering machine, right? But it works because it is so big and so powerful. Individual people standing up to it just get chewed up and spit out. I mean, you are both just going to be put in individual jail cells for a few years—well, Jack, you are going to be in jail for a really long time—and then you'll come back and what? I mean what will have happened? Nothing. The war will go on and your lives will be fucked."

As Phil made his point, I could feel my heart accelerate and a flush rise from my neck to the top of my head. I started in: "No, man, the point is we do have to act as individuals, but we join with others and build a movement. But, yes, it has to start with putting on lives on the line, just like all of us in jail here. We take action. It grows. The resistance builds and they have to stop the wrong they are doing. But it comes from us doing what is right—"

"I mean, what is the alternative, Phil?" Jack asked. "I am not going to have blood on my hands from dropping bombs on a bunch of peasants in Laos." Jack was sitting up, leaning across the bunk, inches from Phil's face.

Phil leaned back, held up his hands and looked back and forth at us. "Whoa, man, whoa! Jeez, you guys are some passionate pacifists, man!" He chuckled tentatively, and I felt myself relax a bit.

"I just mean, I think this is all about power. They have it, we don't. They own everything and we work for them and fight for them. The rich control it all and we have to wake up and band together. We are going to have to fight them, really fight them, not just stop paying taxes or stop registering for the draft"

Jack leaned back against the wall. "Fuck your workers' power crap. You communists are just all talk. The war is real, and it is killing people.

If you are going to be real you have to stand up to the military and not go along. You'll never accomplish a thing, except talk"

I peeked at my watch and saw it was after 10 p.m. An hour had passed since we began talking, and it was time for our space rotation. Together, Jack and I had just given voice to all my core beliefs in a very intense discussion. I felt validated like I hadn't for months.

But Phil made good points, I thought, too. This was not the first time I had heard the critique of pacifism and resistance that Phil had offered, but I came away with a nagging feeling that there was some sense to his ideas. Something about being crammed into jail cells for the last nine or 10 hours made the idea of spending years in jail seem like a pretty bad idea. That and, honestly, it sure didn't seem like we were having much of an impact on Nixon and his war policy despite all our resistance.

Jack and I moved off the lower bunk and stood next to each other at the front of the cell. Phil clambered up onto the top bunk along with another man. After a while, Jack and I sat down on the floor. We slouched away from each other, and I was lucky enough to find a way to rest my head between the bars that was almost comfortable. Our replacements on the bunks shifted around, seeking a comfortable position. The lights were all on in the passageway between the cells, but it began to feel like night as the conversations dwindled. We still had not received any food, and the only water supply was what came out of the single tap in the cell—lukewarm and metal-tasting.

I must have drifted off, because I woke with a start at the loud bang and clang of the main barred door of the cell block being thrown open.

"Get up, GET UP, get UP! You sorry sons-of-bitches! GET UP! You all are moving back to D.C., now GET UP!" A couple dozen sheriff's deputies filed into the cellblock passageway, yelling and banging their night sticks on the cells' bars as they walked past.

One deputy stopped in front of our cell and said, "You fellas line up now as we open the doors and let you out into the hall. Behave yourselves and we'll let you stretch and get a drink and take a piss if you need to on the way out of our jail."

This last bit of information was an unexpected piece of good news for me. I had not screwed up the courage to ask my cellmates to move out of the way so that I could pee in front of all of them in the cell's toilet. Only one of us had.

Glancing at my watch as we lined up, I saw that it was nearly 1:30 a.m. We shuffled out of the cellblock, stopped for our quick drink of water at the water fountain, and then those who needed to were allowed to peel off into a line for the men's restroom as we came into the main entryway. I found myself standing as the last man in the line that slowly snaked forward.

A men's bathroom with three urinals, two stalls, and a set of two porcelain sinks had never looked so good to me. There was a single deputy in the bathroom with the five of us. I stepped up to the splattered, smelly urinal, unzipped, and relaxed as a forceful stream of dark yellow fizzed against the white antiseptic disk in the bottom. I closed my eyes, relaxed, and let out a huge sigh.

"Don't cum in your hand there, faggot! Move your sweet ass!"

"Oh, fuck you," I murmured to myself.

"What did you say, you shit eater?"

"Nothing, nothing, nothing," I said, zipping up and moving toward the sink.

"You bet, nothing, you motherfucker! Now get away from my sink. Step away!" He lifted his billy club up and I backed away, skirting the deputy in a half circle as he turned with me, keeping the club raised, grinning.

"You are the last one in here, little faggot, and I could have some fun with you and this club! Oh, yeah, right up that skinny little ass of yours!" He pushed the head of the club into my stomach lightly. "Yeah!"

I stumbled back and felt the door's handle hit my left hip. I turned quickly, grabbed the handle and flung the door open and rushed through.

He followed me, slapping his left hand with the billy club, yelling "Yeah, yeah, yeah!" and laughing. I moved through the jail lobby as fast as I could, beginning to run, pushed my way through the front doors and rushed to the back of the line of prisoners boarding a bus. The deputy's sinister laughter followed me and he shouted from the front door: "You stay the fuck outta my jail and my county, you cocksucking, queer bastard! And that goes for all y'all, motherfuckers!"

I scurried up the bus steps and took the only open seat as the raucous shouting and laughing continued between the deputies in the parking lot and on the wide sidewalk leading to the jail.

"Man, you OK? What happened in there?" asked my seatmate.

"Yeah, yeah. That was just some crazy fucker in the bathroom. I thought he was going to kill me or something."

"Jesus, well, yeah, they hate us, that's for sure," he agreed.

I nodded. My heart was racing, and I didn't feel like talking. I just wanted to forget the big deputy in the bathroom and how close I had come to, what? A beating? Being raped? I had no idea.

The bus began moving, slowly retracing our route through town and back onto the highway. The humming sound of the tires on the highway, the familiarity of school bus seats and the quiet presence of my comrades from the day of civil disobedience sitting in the darkness around me combined to calm me. We crested a hill coming around a curve and I could see the lights of D.C. in the distance; I could even make out the Washington Monument. Wondering about what was next, I slipped into a sitting doze.

* * *

The bus jerked to a stop and I snapped awake. We were in some sort of underground parking structure and the two buses in front of us were already unloading protesters, who were forming lines outside a set of glass doors 50 feet away. The two deputies in the front of the bus stood and stretched. The door clanked open and one got off as the other turned to us:

"Here we are, boys. D.C.'s jail. Only the finest for the likes of you! Get up and get movin'! On your feet!"

We shuffled slowly down the aisle and off the bus, lining up with the others. I looked around for Jack and Phil, but couldn't find them. Maybe they were on the bus behind us that was just now unloading. I watched as the men stepped off that bus, but had to turn my attention away as we were called to move forward, into the jail.

Once inside, we filed past a glassed-in office, were two deputies controlled the electronically locked barred doors into the cellblock. The locks clicked and our escorts pushed the two doors open for us. As the line snaked inside, we saw an expansive corridor lined with cells slightly larger than the ones we had been in last. The first six cells we passed were filled with standing men, protesters like us, 15 or more in each cell; they were shouting and clapping as we went past. We all joined in a few ragged rounds of *PEACE! NOW* shaking fists or peace signs in the air as we were quickly packed into cells. I was able to squeeze into the front corner of the cell I was in, along with 16 other men and the requisite two metal bunks, sink, and toilet bowl. We stood and chanted while the rest of the protesters were put in the remaining cells.

A sergeant stepped into the middle of the corridor, put his silver whistle between his lips and blew a loud, shrill whistle for what seemed like an eternity. When he mercifully stopped, everyone was quiet, and most of us had our hands over our ears.

"All right, all right, all right!" the sergeant said. "Welcome, welcome to D.C. Metro! You are here as your last stop before arraignment. Arraignment is when you get charged and then you might come back here or not, based on what the judge says, I don't know. Most of y'all is being let go on bail, so maybe you will, maybe not. I don't know.

"What I know is that you in my jail right now. I don't know what time you'll be arraigned, but, don't worry, we'll get you there. It is right upstairs in this building. Now, we know you guys ain't eaten and they tell me some food on the way. I don't know what it is but I'm sure it will taste real good. So, I see you in a while when we bring out the chow." The sergeant turned and walked toward the corridor doorway, the two dozen deputies following behind him.

"Wait, wait! You can't leave us like this! This inhumane! Twenty of us in these cells for two, come on back here, come on!"

The cops kept walking, and the doors clanked shut. A voice came from the front: "We've been here since about six last night. They do come back and take groups out and we guess they are being arraigned. Just, be cool! Take turns sitting and lying down. That's all we can do, man, until we get the fuck outta here!"

I turned away from the corridor and glanced at the men crowded into the cell with me. I didn't recognize anyone. Three men were on each of the two bunks, and the rest of us were standing, about a foot of space between us and the two or three men standing nearby. I was in one of the two front corners of the cell. I backed fully into the corner and slid down the bars until I was sitting.

"I'll sit here for about minutes and then get up and let somebody else have a turn over here. OK?" I asked. A few mumbled something sounding like "OK," and other guys sat down on the floor. In the top bunk, the three men fell into a quiet conversation. I put my head on my crossed arms, leaned on my knees, and closed my eyes.

* * *

Shouting voices, followed by the loud clack of wooden nightsticks hitting cell bars, startled me awake.

"Back AWAY! BACK AWAY from the cell door."

A group of eight deputies were formed in a semicircle around two others who were opening the door of one of the cells quite a ways down the corridor.

"HEY, what's going on down there, man?"

"These pigs are trying to take one of our guys out! These are fuckin' MP PIGS down here, trying to take him out!"

"STEP BACK! STEP BACK, all of you!"

Voices from everywhere in cell block started shouting: "STOP them! NO MPs! No way! STOP the pigs!"

Shouts continued, along with scuffling as the cell door opened, and the cops piled in, pushing the cell's occupants up against bars and bunks. The two MPs emerged with one man, who had gone totally limp, being dragged/carried between them. As they hurried down the corridor past us to a rising chorus of boos and catcalls, I recognized their prisoner.

"JACK! JACK! No, man, no—it's JACK!" I screamed. The MPs moved past quickly, and I thought I saw Jack lifting his head and looking for the person calling his name.

"Hang in there, Jack!" I yelled.

"Who is that guy, man? You know him? What did he do" one of my cellmates asked.

"I just talked to him out in the last jail cell we were in," I explained. "He was in the Air Force, in Turkey, and he quit, man. He walked away. He couldn't keep supporting the war. He just came back home to work against the war."

"Man, he's screwed," another man in the cell chimed in. "I think they must be looking for deserters like him, screening the fingerprints or something. Maybe they have a list of AWOLs, deserters, resisters of various sorts," he continued.

"You think?" I nearly choked on my words.

"Yeah, yeah, well, maybe," he continued. "I mean they've had us all for, what, about fourteen, fifteen hours now. You think they wouldn't be looking for people they want?"

"I guess, I guess. It's just that, well, Jack, I mean, jeez, I don't know. Shit, shit, shit." I hung my head and found myself blinking back tears.

"What, man, are you, like, in the same situation or whatever?" he asked.

I took a deep breath. "No, well … I don't know. I, uh, well, not a deserter. I'm a draft resister. Never registered. Made a big public deal of it at conservative church meeting."

"Well, that is different, I think. I mean, I don't know, not a lawyer or anything, man. But, have the cops or the feds interviewed you or investigated what you did, I mean, as far as you know?"

"No, not that I know of. But who knows?"

"True, true. It could be going on and they just haven't decided to talk to you or whatever, not yet. Who knows how they do these things. But, if you were indicted for something, you would know it, you know? I mean, if there was a warrant for you and stuff. And that guy, there, uh—"

"Jack?" I offered.

"Yeah, Jack. I mean there must be military paper out on him, you know? That's why the MPs came. It sucks, it really sucks. But, it doesn't sound like your situation, you know?"

"Makes sense. Yeah, OK, OK … yeah."

"I'm Fred, by the way. Just came over here from Philadelphia."

"I'm Paul. Chicago."

We drifted into small talk, then silence. I looked at my watch. It was just after 4 a.m.

Once more, I dozed off, only to be startled awake when the main cell door squealed as it opened and slammed into the wall. I craned my head over my shoulder and saw three guards pushing a large cart stacked with cartons of milk and individual sandwiches wrapped in plastic. Stopping at each cell, they passed the sandwiches and milk through the bars to eagerly grabbing hands.

"One each, one each!" they told us. "Don't have enough 'cept for one milk and one sammich each!"

When they reached our cell, those of us in the front reached out and took all the sandwiches they would give us and passed them back to our comrades. I ripped the plastic off a sandwich and took a huge bite: bologna on white bread never tasted so good! The sandwich was gone in a few seconds, followed by the milk. I hadn't realized how hungry I was, but then remembered my last meal had been breakfast yesterday.

I stood up and shifted places with a guy who had been standing a while. I leaned against a corner of one of the bunks and tried to relax in the crowded space. The food had gotten everyone up, and for 15minutes, a low conversational buzz—punctuated by occasional laughs and shouts—filled the jail. Slowly, the conversations petered out and quiet settled over the cellblock again. I was so tired that I swayed on my feet with my eyes closed and my mind totally adrift. The minutes dragged on and on.

Another screech and slam from the main gate announced the re-entry of the guards.

"Listen up! Listen up!" said one of the guards. "It's your lucky day! Time to go to court you guys, time for court. We are going to take you out one group at a time and take you upstairs. We will take you to a holding cell outside your courtroom. Then you will be taken in for your arraignment."

Everyone began talking at once as the guards opened the first cell and escorted the men through the gate and down the hall. While we waited in our cell, those of us who wanted to took turns using the toilet and the tiny sink next to it. As I took my turn at the sink and splashed lukewarm water on my face, I wondered exactly where I was in the city and how I would reconnect with my friends.

As good as their word, the guards returned and emptied another cell, then another, and another. It took 45 minutes for the guards to reach our cell and open the door. We shuffled out and down the wide corridor, past guards, and policemen looking out at us through their interior hallway windows. As we approached the elevator, my step quickened, and I held my head up. A change of scene and the hope of getting out of jail without being turned over to the FBI were energizing for me.

The freight elevator's doors were open, waiting for us, along with an older man sitting on a stool in the corner in a guard's uniform.

"Step right in! Step in and fill 'er up," the guard said. "You all are friends, don't be bashful, come on, ain't no other ride comin' for y'all." Once we all got in with the three guards standing at the front facing us holding their nightsticks, he closed the doors. The elevator jumped a couple of times and then began to move up. "Man, y'all ripe, too!" he exclaimed. "Phew-eeeeee! Don't y'all know you s'posed to clean up for the judge? Je-SUS, you worse than the last group! I like to die 'fore gettin' all y'all up to court today. Should pay me hazard pay today, don't you think, Sarge?"

"Sheeeeet! You want hazard pay, you come down in the cells with us," Sarge said. "Like the elephant house down there! Smell just like the zoo with all these guys down there in holding."

The elevator bumped to a stop. The door opened and the guards backed into a bright hallway, motioning us to get off and move to the right.

"Enjoy your court day, boys!" the elevator guard told us. "You'll be waiting on Judge Simmons. Old Judge Simmons, he do you right with your smelly selves. Let me go and get me some Lysol spray or somethin', damn! How many more loads I gotta take of these, Sarge? Jesus, have mercy!"

We were in a service hallway that ended at a set of sturdy wooden doors. The sergeant took a key ring from his belt and shuffled through a dozen or so keys, before selecting one and pushing it into the lock. He turned the key, opened both doors, and motioned us inside. It was a 12-by-18-foot room with no windows. Locker room-type benches lined the walls.

"Take a seat on the bench. Come on. Move along here, take a seat. There is plenty of room. OK, OK, now listen up. In a while you are going before Judge Julius Simmons, D.C. District Court. This is your arraignment. In other words, you are being formally charged. Y'all have attorneys representing you. They are out there now with another group. They will be in here shortly to talk with you. We are going to leave you now as soon as a bailiff comes in from the court."

A minute later, the door on the other side of the room opened, and a tall, thin older white man in a sheriff's uniform walked in. "Ok, Sarge, I got 'em," he said. "Thanks."

"See ya, then, with the next group. Gonna be a long day."

The guards exited, pulling the doors shut behind them and sending the deadbolt home with a loud click. The bailiff crossed the room and tested the doors, then crossed back and stood silently in front of the courtroom door. I sighed, wondering silently about how much longer this would be, slouched against the wall, and closed my eyes.

A loud knock on the courtroom-side door startled me awake. I rolled my shoulders and cracked my stiff neck, glancing at my watch. I thought I had forgotten to wind it or something because it looked like it was stuck at midnight—it couldn't be noon already! I held my wrist up to my ear and heard the rapid tick-tock. I was feeling totally lost as the short woman in a rumpled suit walked into the room.

"Bailiff, thank you." she said. "I would like to meet with my clients." She watched as he nodded and exited.

"I'm Mary Gleason from the ACLU here in D.C. I am a volunteer and am your court-appointed lawyer. I am going to pass around a clipboard where I need you to print your name, date of birth, address and phone number. I will then go out and we will match you with the list of arrest records we have. Once we have everybody confirmed, we will let Judge Simmons know. We will have you come into the courtroom as a group and sit in the jury box. The judge will come in and start the proceedings. When your name is called, stand up. Affirm it is your name. I will plead you all not guilty. We already have raised money for you, and you will be released on bail. You will each have to do that and then the proceeding will end.

The judge will leave and then you will be called up by the clerk to sign your name. Then you can go. Any questions?"

We shuffled in our seats, trying to get our minds working. For the last 24 hours, things had moved so slowly and now they seemed to be moving quickly. The clipboard made its way to me and I began printing out my particulars, half-listening to my comrades' questions and answers. The gist of the back and forth was that the organizers were well-prepared for handling this part of the May Day event. We were being charged with a misdemeanor offense and did not need to return for trial unless we wanted to. Mary said that she expected there would be some legal effort to get all of the charges dismissed, but that the legal strategy was not fully developed yet. We would be kept informed and could be involved to the extent we wanted to.

After answering everyone's questions, Mary collected the clipboard and knocked on the courtroom door. As Mary exited the room, she told us it wouldn't be much longer. We slumped back on the benches. Time crawled forward again as we waited for the door to open for the last act of the drama that had begun the afternoon before with our arrest at the Justice Department.

The door opened about half an hour later and the bailiff stepped into the room. "I am going to call you in groups of eight," he said. "You are to line up and follow me into the courtroom. You will sit in the jury box and wait for the clerk to call your name, then you go up and stand by your lawyer in front of the Judge. He will ask the questions and you will let your lawyer do the talkin' unless she says different. Got it?"

There were murmurs of agreement.

"OK, first group, here you go." The names were called, and the first group left. The bailiff returned about five minutes later and called another group. That process repeated itself three times until they finally my name. I stood in line, tucked in my shirt, ran my fingers through my hair and straightened my glasses.

We were led to the jury box and found seats, looking out on what had become a mass production operation to efficiently empty the jails and fight the court battles another day. I scanned the courtroom and, in addition to the older Black man in black robes sitting behind his raised dais at the front, there were a bevy of clerks, bailiffs and lawyers moving quickly between tables in the front. The back half of the room was lined with 10 rows of wooden benches that were half-filled with people—two of whom were waving at me! Somehow, some way, Joe and Pauline were there! I grinned from ear to ear and waved back to them as relief washed through my tired body.

The sharp rap of the judge's gavel brought my attention back to the front of the room.

"Clerk continue with the next prisoner," the judge said.

"Gregory Logan." A man in front of me stood up and walked over to stand alongside Mary .

"Is your name Gregory Logan?"

"Yes, your Honor."

"You are charged with unlawful assembly and refusing to obey a police officer. How do you plead?'

"He pleads not guilty, your Honor," Mary answered.

"$250 bail. Court date to be determined," the judge said and again the gavel fell. "Next."

This process repeated itself over and over. My attention shifted back and forth between the proceedings and Joe and Pauline. Soon, my name was called.

I stepped in front of the Judge and affirmed who I was when asked. He didn't look away from the paper on his desk as he read the charges and set bail. I caught Mary's eye and mouthed "thank you" as I walked over to the clerk's table. After signing an agreement to return for my trial, I bounded through the low gates separating the courtroom from the spectators' benches and embraced Pauline and Joe. We hung on to each other and barged through the doors into the hallway outside.

"OH, MAN! It is SO GOOD to see you guys!" I said. "JESUS CHRIST! I never thought I was getting out, oh, MAN, how did you know how to find me? Did you wait a long time? OH, MAN, OH, MAN, OH, MAN it is so great to see you two!"

We made our way down the hall, found an exit stairway, and raced laughingly down four flights of stairs, tumbling out the door into the street. We held on to each other as we made our way down the street to the car. Pauline drove as Joe explained how they had both been taken to the D.C. jail, released last night, then made their way back to Word of Life. After they got up this morning, they had found that the May Day Organizing Committee had set up an information center with details on those of us still in jail and our expected court hearings in terms of both time and location. It was amazing to us that the D.C. jail system was that organized!

They told me that the protests, although originally planned to continue throughout the week, were pretty much over. Most folks were not interested in continuing civil disobedience after being released from jail. Small, spontaneous protests continued, but nothing on the scale of the Justice Department sit-in or Monday's traffic stoppages were planned. As we pulled into the church's parking lot, we had resolved to let me sleep a few hours and then head out for Detroit after rush hour.

I found my sleeping bag in the basement and collapsed into it, asleep before my head touched my rolled up jean jacket that served as a pillow. The next thing I knew, Lyndy was rubbing my shoulders and telling me it was time to go. I managed to crawl out of the sleeping bag, stumble to the bathroom and find my way to the back seat of the car. Bob took the first turn at the wheel, as the rest of us waved goodbye to the pastor and a handful of our erstwhile protest comrades. Pauline graciously let me rest my head on her shoulder. I awoke when the car stopped at a truck stop somewhere in Pennsylvania.

It was nearly 10:30 a.m. when we got back to the car after fortifying ourselves on pancakes, eggs and coffee. I took the next shift driving while Joe claimed shotgun and took up his endless quest to find good music. After about 20 minutes, the backseat contingent of Pauline, Bob and Lyndy fell asleep. Joe cracked his vent window and lit up a Winston that we shared in silence. The miles hummed by as the country music station Joe had selected played softly.

After a few more miles the radio was playing more static than music, so I flicked it off. Except for the sounds of the engine and the highway, all was silent in the car. I found myself thinking about Jack, the Air Force deserter, imagining that he was already in a military jail, facing an indefinite future of court martial, a long prison sentence, and an uncertain future beyond that. I realized I was incredibly relieved that I had not been discovered as a non-registrant, relieved that I wasn't facing what Jack was at that moment. I felt incredibly guilty that I was so relieved, but as I turned the events of the last few days over and over again in my mind, I couldn't deny the feeling of being lucky, or privileged—or both.

Before May Day, I realized, I hadn't really come to grips with the impact my resistance would have on me and my future. I had read about conscientious objectors in prison and had talked to a few, but this had given me a small taste—a little more than 24 hours—of what I really was going to lose if I were arrested and convicted for draft resistance. I had a new, visceral sense of the potential for violence being done to me by guards and the absolute loss of meaningful control over my activities—the loss of freedom.

The May Day experience also forced me to revisit the arguments around the effectiveness and impact of nonviolent direct action. I found myself reflecting on the forceful arguments Phil had made in the discussions with Jack and I in the jail cell, about the futility of our individually based, conscientious actions in the face of the monstrosity of the U.S. war machine. Earlier, at the truck stop, we had discussed our disappointments with the May Day action: that fewer protesters came than we had hoped; that the government workforce did not join the protest in any discernible way; that, despite the excitement and disruption caused by the Monday morning traffic disruptions and the Tuesday sit-in, the liberal "establishment" voices of the media patronized us, and the Nixon Administration seemed more determined than ever to destroy Vietnam.

My thoughts flew along with the miles as I followed the highway north and west. I was beginning to look for another truck stop to get gas and coffee, when Joe jerked awake with a start. Seemingly disoriented, he took off his glasses, rubbed his eyes, and put his glasses back on.

"Oh, yeah, now I remember. Haven't you got us home yet? Fuck, man, I gotta piss."

CHAPTER 7:
DISILLUSIONED DISCIPLE

"**H**ot off the presses! Peace, Scott," read the note attached to 10 booklets in a package that was waiting for me in the pile of mail at our apartment when Joe and I returned from Washington. *Check Out the Odds! If You're Not in the Lottery Your Number Can't Come Up* had been authored and published by a loose collective of Minneapolis draft resisters to promote non-registration. I was one of the contributors, and my quotes were featured, along with a half dozen others', throughout the booklet.

While skimming the text and re-reading what I had written, I reflected that my 19th birthday was around the corner. Almost a year had passed since I had publicly announced my draft resistance and there was no evidence that the FBI or any Federal prosecutor had noticed my non-registration. I wondered if that would change now when some FBI informant passed on the booklet to one of the field offices or headquarters, and they opened an investigation. Further, the booklet was material evidence of at least two more felonies on my part: conspiring to undermine the selective service and directly advocating draft resistance. With the memory of the D.C. jail so fresh in my mind, I gulped and took a deep breath. Deciding I'd better read the booklet from cover to cover before the FBI did, I flopped down on the ratty brown couch in our living room, lit a cigarette, and began to read.

I stopped short when I read Scott Sandvik's personal addendum to the collective's introduction (this section was formatted as this poem):

I've changed in the way I look at my nonregistration

I used to consider myself locked into a certain response

> *to the draft*

and to the process of prosecution which would follow

I realize that I have to stay flexible

and meet situations as they present themselves

Trying in each case to do as much as I can do the

> *right thing*

realizing that I am human, that I have my limitations,

> *and that*

some of the consequences of my actions could prove very

> *destructive for me*

I'm not out to destroy myself

I see that this struggle is gonna be a lifelong thing

and I should pace myself accordingly

being careful not to burn myself out at such a young age

I am open to the possibility of ...registering

After a few additional paragraphs of explanation, Scott went on to conclude his personal addendum to the introduction by saying:

... So where I'm at now is that I'm thinking of registering if I get indicted. This may make you wonder why I'm working on a book on non-registration—you may think it's a contradiction—but I don't. What I think is most important is not whether a guy is registered or not, but rather that,

in choosing a course to take in relation to the draft, he be honest with himself and choose the path which best fits him, taking into account his various commitments, responsibilities and limitations. Hopefully in doing this he'll be able to keep himself out of the military ... I realize how few of the answers I have and am trying to open up to be able to learn from others.

I threw the booklet down on the couch, shaken to my core by the combination of Scott's apparent change of heart combined with my own experiences of the last week in the May Day demonstrations and the nights in jail. I pulled on my shoes and stormed out the front door of the apartment, calling over my shoulder to Joe that I'd be back in a while. I spent the next hour or so pounding my way through the grid of Maywood's streets while I wrestled with variations of the question "now what?" I found no easy answers that afternoon as I strode through Maywood's neighborhoods. Instead, I pushed my questions aside and threw myself into the rhythms of our work both in the church and in our neighborhood to stop the war and support racial justice.

* * *

As the crowd of parishioners shook hands with, and then filed past, Father Mike into the bright sunshine outside of Our Lady of Perpetual Help, they were slowed by the sight of Joe and me walking in wide circles around their modernistic statue of Jesus in the small plaza in front of the church. We had our arms spread wide and were humming as low and loud as we could, interrupting our humming every few seconds by shouting "BOOM!" "BOOM!" "BOOM!" We stepped over and around four of our erstwhile comrades from the West Suburban Alliance Against War and Racism who were splayed unmoving on the sidewalk, playing the part of dead Vietnamese villagers, the victims of Joe's and my B-52 bombers. Two other members of the Alliance passed out flyers about the People's Peace Treaty while a third shouted out a variety of short messages along the lines of: "Nixon is lying to us! He said he would stop the war, but he has just started the bombing again! Hundreds of Vietnamese and Americans are dying every week in this pointless, unjust war. It's up to us to stop the war and we can do it through the Peoples' Peace Treaty. Read all about it! The People's Peace Treaty—WE can STOP the WAR in Vietnam!"

This was our second church of the day, and our guerilla theatre troop planned to hit one more before we wrapped up. We traded off playing different parts in the sketch, which usually lasted no more than 10 minutes, as no one usually paused too long or stayed behind to talk to us. Still, almost everyone took our leaflets and our group felt like these actions were effective in building awareness of the Peoples' Peace Treaty.

This was just one of the ways that Joe and I were spending numerous hours on antiwar efforts each week in and around Maywood and other near western suburbs of Chicago. During any given week that spring and early summer, we could be found leafleting high schools; selling copies of the *Peoples' Voice*—a locally produced, radical newspaper that always had a focus on the war in each issue—at the gates of a number of large factories; and, most recently, going door-to-door in the residential neighborhoods of small bungalows, seeking signatures on petitions addressed to Congress with the text of the Peoples' Peace Treaty. We felt welcomed and befriended by a number of local, activist families—the Elberts, the Lumpkins, the Hilperts—and had a widening social network that ranged from the radical Marxists of *Peoples' Voice* to the "house church" community that met sporadically for potluck dinners and folk music-based worship services at the Elberts' home.

Inspired by Walther League members and friends, some of whom had expanded an existing residential community in Hyde Park and others who established a new community in Wilmette, Joe and I had convinced five others to join us in establishing a similar intentional residential community in Maywood. Two of our potential community members were Walther League executive director Mark Hellman and his wife, Anne Rist. Anne and Mark had recently married and decided it was time to be practical and buy a house. They had started looking at homes in Maywood earlier in the year and now had a contract on a home that we all thought could meet our needs. The sale was contingent, though, on Anne and Mark obtaining a zoning variance that would allow more than three unrelated people to live in one residence. Given that Maywood was a majority African-American town, many of whose residents had been victims of housing discrimination in the recent past, and we were all white, we felt that it was important that we play by the rules in buying the house. We were waiting for a late June planning board hearing on the proposed variance.

In the meantime, Joe and I moved from our very dilapidated and roach-infested apartment above the storefronts in downtown Maywood to a well-maintained, basement apartment in a seven-unit building across the street from Bethlehem Lutheran Church. A church member owned the building, and we were able to move in for significantly reduced rent in exchange for agreeing to cut the grass, sweeping and cleaning the common spaces, and being an on-site presence for the owner.

We spent some time each week focused on what we considered to be our church-specific work. This included maintaining very active correspondence with youth leaders and pastors throughout the region, especially with the groups in Superior, Stevens Point and Milwaukee, Wisconsin, in St. Louis, Missouri, as well as with groups in multiple suburbs of Chicago. Although we were not actively pushing programs like the Hunger Hikes that the League had started in 1968, we served as resources, suggesting books and movies that could be used to build awareness, particularly of racism and the war. We also planned and delivered weekend experiential/ educational programs—"live-ins"—with and for the groups we were working with around the region.

I had also taken on the responsibility of chairing the planning committee for a Walther League national gathering that would take place in Milwaukee a few days in advance of the Synod's biennial convention being held there in July. We hoped to convene at least 100 young, largely white young people at the same time as our partners in Black Youth Unlimited (BYU) convened their own members. We were planning some joint worship and dialogue activities with BYU during our meetings. We were also planning joint awareness-building and—potentially—protest events with BYU, as well as a group of pastors and seminarians who were increasingly alienated from the Synod's leadership around both internal church doctrine disputes and lack of social action. The convention-related group had loosely affiliated into a coalition that was calling itself "Moving through Milwaukee."

As my 19th birthday came and went, and the gathering and convention grew closer, the pace of planning meetings, phone calls, and visits to Milwaukee quickened and left me little time to wrestle with the questions that had been gnawing at me since May Day. Without really knowing why, I felt increasingly on edge, worried about all that I was responsible for, and driven to a frenetic pace to get everything prepared. By July 4—when Joe and I headed up to Milwaukee to join the rest of the League staff and kick off the gathering the next morning—I was ready but feeling more ready to have the whole event—and the Synod convention—behind me.

Immediately after our Milwaukee Walther League Gathering and the Synod's convention, I took off by myself and headed for Michigan's Warren Dunes State Park on the southeastern shore of Lake Michigan. There I quickly discovered how physically out of shape I had become. On my third afternoon in the park, I stopped climbing just halfway up a massive dune and feeling totally wasted and winded as sweat poured into my eyes. The sand gave way even more as I paused, gravity and the weight of my body starting my slow slide back the way I had come.

"Fuck this, you wimp!" I mumbled to myself—though I could have shouted it since no one else seemed to be around in this far northern section of the park. I took my hat off, mopped my forehead with a soaked, sandy kerchief, slammed my hat back on over my mess of wet hair, and then leaned in to continue the climb. Step after slippery step, panting all the way, I finally made it to the top of the dune I had picked out from my walk along the beach below. It was by no means the highest dune in the park—those were further south, nearer the campsites where all the people were—but it was at least 100 feet up, I thought. I collapsed in a heap on a patch of grass and tried to catch my breath. There was no shade. But as I pushed myself up to sitting and turned west toward the sparkling lake, a steady breeze cooled me as I sipped water from my canteen and caught my breath.

"It's the fucking cigarettes, I guess," I grumbled aloud. "Gotta stop that shit soon."

I never had been in the habit of talking to myself out loud before, but since I had gotten to the park and pitched my little pup tent two nights back, I found myself spontaneously verbalizing some of my random thoughts. I didn't think about it much but when I did, I just thought about the fact that this was probably the longest time in my life that I had been nearly completely alone— and that I was missing human contact. There certainly were other people in the park, but I had taken pains to avoid them. Since it was the middle of the week when I arrived, I had found a campsite that was isolated. I purposefully walked away from the crowded beaches and dunes during my rambling walks and found empty stretches, or places where I could only see a handful of people in the distance. While swimming by myself did not seem like a smart idea, I had waded out into the water and played in the waves.

I lay back again and squinted up at the sky. I thought it was probably mid-afternoon by now, given the angle of the sun and the fact that I was getting a little hungry. I had taken off on this hike after eating a peanut butter and jelly sandwich and an apple at my campsite. I began wondering exactly what I had left to eat. I grinned, thinking how shocked my parents would be at the idea of how little I had done to plan and prepare for this camping trip. During my childhood, seven to 10 days of camping in the national forest campgrounds in Missouri was our typical family vacation every summer. My parents were list makers and great planners—and I supposed they had to be if they were taking five kids of a wide age range to the woods, lakes, and streams for more than a week at a time.

This trip had been totally spur-of-the-moment. I had come back from 10 days in Milwaukee completely burned out. Joe and I had driven back from Milwaukee together to our Broadview apartment and had been at each other's throats for the entire three-hour trip. That afternoon, I told him I was going to get away for a while and go up to Michigan and do some camping. He said he had no interest in camping and would just hang at the apartment. The next morning, I threw the pup tent, some clothes, my sleeping bag, and whatever food I could find, in the car and took off. I had a full tank of gas and about 15 dollars in my pocket, but even with a VW bug, I wasn't going to go very far. That's how I ended up at Warren Dunes State Park with a little less than a half-tank of gas and maybe six dollars left. I knew I was going to have to leave soon, since I didn't have enough money to get more than another night of camping and still have enough gas to get home. I was also down to my last five cigarettes and had very little food. I would likely have to miss a few meals unless I left the next morning.

I sat up, combed my tangled hair with my fingers, and pushed my hat back on my head, pulling the brim down to shade my eyes from the sun's dazzling rays bouncing off the lake. I turned my thoughts away from the practical issues of my impulsive camping trip and toward the issues that had been circulating again and again through my mind since Milwaukee. For two full days now, I had hiked for miles along the beach, trudged up and run down dozens of dunes, and sat still for hours on end day and night, losing myself in the sensations of breeze, sky, water, sand, screeching gulls and lapping waves. My mind turned, again and again, to three issues that I felt I had to resolve: my draft resistance, life beyond Walther League, and love relationships.

My thoughts almost always started with my draft resistance and what would come next. For the most part, I felt confident and proud of myself for taking a stand, for putting my body where my beliefs, my faith, and my heart all seemed to demand it. I was still convinced that individuals taking such stands—despite the risks to individual liberty—might make all the difference, ultimately, in life writ large (and small). But as confident as I felt, I was also unsure that such individual acts of conscience mattered as much as building a mass social movement that could change power dynamics in society. I thought about what Scott had written in his introduction to *Check Out the Odds,* and what I had been hearing and reading from my new friends who were committed Marxists, about what it took to change society. Their view meant taking a very long view of social change that, in my mind, discounted the role of individual acts of conscience. It wasn't that these acts didn't matter. It was more that I didn't think they might be as important as I had been thinking they were when I decided to resist the draft. This was because the powerful, I now believed, would only make change based on the countervailing power of the many, not singular acts of conscience and defiance.

It was hard to untangle my thinking about individual conscience and social change from my growing frustration and disillusionment with the response of the church—in particular, my own church, the Missouri Synod—to the movement for peace and justice. For three years now, I had worked with the church as the primary focus of my energy for two basic reasons. First, that our common belief in the Gospel of Jesus must lead us all to conclude that we had to act to break the "hunger chain" of linked "-isms"—racism, militarism, sexism—that impoverished so many people and caused suffering and death. Second, that the church, once awakened and mobilized, would be a massive force for reordering society toward justice and peace.

But my own experiences over the past year working for the Walther League was leading me to doubt myself. Top of mind were the experiences I had had in the prior two weeks across the lake in Milwaukee. Not only was the attendance at our League national gathering disappointing—we fell well short of our goal of having more than 100 attendees—it seemed like our message was not really resonating in the way that it had in 1968 and '69 when thousands of kids from hundreds of churches participated in Hikes for the Hungry across the country. Our increasing focus on tackling racism as we had with our gathering's theme in Milwaukee—White and Young in Today's Church and Society—was a hard sell. While we as a national staff were completely committed and felt we were effective with the small number of kids we did reach, this was no national-scale movement. We had begun to worry out loud with each other about our dwindling numbers and the lack of major, unifying activities like the Hunger Hikes.

Further complicating matters was the Missouri Synod's growing conservative movement, which had taken over the presidency of the Synod in 1969 and now was moving to consolidate its power in the districts, seminaries, and teachers' colleges. While this movement was based in a fundamentalist and dogmatic approach to the church's teaching that didn't seem to matter to anyone outside the church, the movement was socially and politically conservative, as well.

The Walther League, since its founding in the 1890s, had often found itself crosswise with Synod leaders. The new conservative movement saw us as a perfect target for mobilizing their troops—a means by which to test their messages and political tactics, as well as gauge their growing strength. More than a dozen churches and districts had submitted resolutions to the convention condemning the League and calling for a variety of sanctions against it, including ending official recognition of the League as an auxiliary of the Synod and another that sought a theological investigation of it . While all these resolutions were successfully blocked at the convention, a new, compromise resolution was passed, calling upon a powerful internal committee of the Synod to define the role and relationship of the League to the Church. We had conducted—and won—a defensive, tactical victory at the Milwaukee convention. But it had left me feeling besieged and worn down, more convinced than ever that instead of being a place of kindred spirits who supported each other in the battles against evil in the world, my church community was controlled by men concerned with fostering their own power and control over others. They were, in a word, hypocrites.

I was pretty much done with them, I thought, as I stood up on the dune and stretched. "Just. Not. Worth. Energy," I said aloud as I began stepping down the dune, the momentum quickly carrying me forward into a run. I began puffing and chanting "Not. Worth. Energy. Not. Worth. Energy," as I careened down the slope. When I reached the flat expanse of the beach, I slowed enough to kick off my sneakers, throw my hat and glasses down, strip off my T-shirt, and rush into the water.

The water deepened very gradually, and I was 20 yards offshore before I dived into a wave and took a dozen strokes out into the lake. I stopped and pulled my feet under me to check for the bottom and barely touched the sand, so I turned and swam parallel with the shore for a while, and then turned over and floated on my back. The water felt incredibly cold after the hot sun on the dune, and I shivered a little as my body adjusted. I kicked my feet and pulled myself along slowly with my arms as I squinted up at the deep blue of the sky. I let the waves push me in toward shore for a while, and then used my lazy backstroke to recover the distance back into the lake. I repeated this process a few times. As I floated and felt the water's rhythm, I watched little white clouds move slowly across the sky and listened to the pulsing of my heart in my ears. Time slowed as I floated. Finally, I felt like I was getting too cold and flipped over to swim to shore. As I did, I noticed a man standing next to what I thought was probably my things, watching me. He was all in white—from his slouchy, white fisherman's cap to his T-shirt and trunks—and waved at me when he noticed I had seen him. I wondered what exactly he was doing there as I swam into shore and then walked up through the shallows onto the beach.

"What's happenin'?" I said, wiping the water off my face and pushing my hair back with my hands. He was smiling and held my hat and glasses out toward me. Up close, I could see he seemed to be in his late 20sor early 30s. I immediately typed him as some kind of businessman.

"Hi. I guess these are yours. Sorry, I don't have a towel or anything," he said.

"It's OK." I picked up my T-shirt and shook it out, then used it to wipe off my face and chest. I put on my glasses and hat and looked over at the man more closely, not sure what exactly this was all about.

"I'm sorry, I don't mean to freak you out," he said. "I was just walking up the beach and saw you swimming, so I stopped. It looked like you were having a great time out there. Very relaxing, I guess."

"Yeah. It was. Felt good after being out in the sun and climbing the dunes and everything." I picked up my shoes and started slowly walking back toward the campground about a mile away. He surprised me by walking along with me.

It had never been easy for me to talk with strangers, but nearly three days of self-imposed isolation motivated me. Combined with his easygoing manner and apparent interest in me, we struck up a conversation. "Look, I mean I know I look very, what, straight?" he said. "Is that what you guys say, now, like as opposed to hippies and freaks—"

"Like me," I grinned.

He laughed. "Yeah. I mean, you dress the part, man. Anyway, back in my college days I was more like you are, long hair and everything. I was in school, you know, keeping my II-S deferment, and Karen—she's my wife—and I started going to the teach-ins and stuff about Vietnam. I started at the seminary to keep getting the deferment and, well, because I liked thinking and talking about God and all the issues, you know. But we weren't careful enough and got pregnant. Well, one thing led to another and we're married for six years, have kids. I was lucky enough to not get drafted, but I had to drop out of seminary and work. Yeah, things happen fast sometimes. I don't think I even blinked, and, well, here I am."

We walked on in a silence that was punctuated by the background cacophony of the seagulls' cries. I had a feeling I could really talk to this guy, but didn't know where to start, since I was jam-packed with thoughts and feelings that I had been processing and re-processing alone for the last few days.

"What's your name, man?" I asked

"Gabe. Well, Gabriel, but I go by Gabe."

"I'm Paul. Good to meet you." We shook hands and then continued walking. I gave a somewhat meandering account of my last two days, what the Walther League was and some of the issues I had been thinking about. Maybe because he had talked about his path to marriage and fatherhood, I surprised myself by veering more into my confusion about my relationship with Jeanne Boeh, another Walther League staff member and editor of our newspaper. We had had what seemed to me to be a confusing sexual encounter during the last night of the convention. We found ourselves bedding down for the night in the same corner of the church basement that a dozen or so staffers and other League activists had used as headquarters during the Synod convention. Talking led to tentative and then passionate kissing that usually would have led, in my previous experience with others, to sex. Jeanne gave clear signals that she did not want to have sex that night and when I asked her if she wanted to stop, she said yes, and so we did. The next afternoon, before she left with a group of other staff and volunteers for a six-week service and learning trip to Guatemala, we fumbled around with each other again. I professed my attraction and what I was sure was the beginning of love to her, and she was not at all in the same emotional or mental state about me. She had been gone for almost two weeks now, and I had been replaying these events repeatedly in my mind. I had not even talked to Joe about all of it before I took off for Warren Dunes. It was a relief to unburden myself to Gabe.

"Wow! That is quite the story there, Paul." He paused. I thought to myself that I had probably said too much too fast. I knew I could be intense at times and could be off-putting. We walked on in silence for half a minute. My heart sank when I saw that we were coming up on the path that led off to the campground and would likely go our separate ways soon.

Gabe waded into the water a ways and then looped back toward me, stopping just in front of me so that I had to stop walking. He looked me dead in the eye.

"Man, you've got a lot going on," he said. "I mean your job sounds intense. Then you have the draft and the war. You didn't say exactly what your status is, but it's got to be hitting you, I mean, it does all the guys your age. Then your friend, Jeanne, yeah, a lot there to sort through, too. I guess all I can say is, really, be easy on yourself. Just try to be in this place, this beauty, and let it soak in for a while." He smiled and turned back toward the lake, lifting his arms and motioning. "It's good just to be, really be *here* right now."

He started walking slowly again. I stood where I was for a few moments and watched the waves roll in, the sun edging closer to the horizon, the water sparkling. I caught up with Gabe just before the path to the campground turned away from the beach and toward the woods.

"Thanks, Gabe. Thanks for listening," I said. "I will take your advice."

"Oh, sure, I mean, I hope it helps," he said. "Sometimes just having somebody to talk to, you know."

I nodded and pointed to the sign that read "Campground" and said, "I'm down here. I don't have much more than water, but you are welcome to come over and sit at the picnic table and have a drink if you want."

"Thanks, but I really better get back and make sure the boys haven't driven Karen nuts, you know! We're down at the next bunch of campsites." Gabe held out his hand, and we shook. "I'll maybe catch you later. Or tomorrow."

"Cool."

I turned and started walking toward the campground, thinking again about what Gabe had said. I needed to be easy on myself. And just *be*. My anxiety melted a little, and I felt more peaceful than I had in weeks—maybe even months, given all that had happened from May Day on. At the top of a slight rise, I turned back toward the lake and scanned the beach for Gabe, thinking maybe I could wave, but he was already gone. The next morning I gathered up my gear and headed back to Chicago.

* * *

"No rent for rats! No rent for rats! No rent for rats!" We all shouted in unison with Marcus Salone as he led the picket line holding a megaphone in one hand and, in the other, a homemade sign with our main slogan—"No rent for rats!"—scrawled in red and black across it. It was just about noon on a sunny Saturday in early October, and 15 of us were following Marcus, the president of the newly formed Austin Tenants Association, in a circle on the sidewalk in front of the Coates-Miller Real Estate office on Madison Street. A squad car was parked right in front of the office, and two bulky, uniformed Chicago cops slouched against the front of it, glaring at us. Horns sounded and folks waved at us from their passing cars.

I caught up to Jeanne, who was walking right in front of me in the line. Not too bad for our first action, huh?" I said.

She smiled. "Yeah, I guess. But where are the tenants from the actual Coates-Miller buildings? It looks like mainly us and the *Peoples' Voice* crowd."

She was right, of course. Counting the two of us, more than half the picket line was young and white, at least four of whom—Joyce, Mike, Al and Joe K—were part of *Peoples' Voice*. I was pretty sure that most Coates-Millers tenants in the Austin neighborhood were Black. And while parts of Austin were still majority white or even somewhat integrated in 1971, that was changing rapidly. Chicago was the most segregated city in the northern United States for a reason—in a word, "redlining." Housing, economic, and education policy all aligned to support racial segregation and white supremacy; when Blacks began integrating neighborhoods, the policymakers and power brokers moved their levers and re-segregated neighborhoods quickly. One of those levers was lack of housing code enforcement, especially in rental properties like those owned by big companies like Coates-Miller. Thus, the Austin Tenants Association had been founded just a few months earlier.

I fell back in line behind Jeanne and joined the chanting. As we circled, my mind wandered back a few months to my return from my solo camping trip. I had been greeted not just by Joe, but by our new roommate, Nathan Gardels. He was the new staffer who was replacing Jeanne as editor of the Walther League monthly newspaper, *Bridge*. I had met Nathan briefly before, but now had the chance to spend much more time with him. The three of us soon became fast friends, spending hours in the evenings smoking the unfiltered French cigarettes Nathan favored, drinking tea and coffee, and debating all manner of issues and events, ranging from liberation theology to the arrest and pending trial of Eqbal Ahmed and the other members of the Harrisburg 7.

The Maywood Planning Board had convened in early August and voted to deny the zoning variance for Mark and Anne's house. They decided not to purchase the property, and that they would not join the rest of us in pursuing alternative housing to establish our collective. The six of us ended up renting two adjacent first-floor apartments in the Austin neighborhood—becoming the Austin Collective instead of the Maywood Collective when we moved into the apartments October 1. We were now at the end of our first month living together, and it all felt a little disjointed to me. We had not taken any steps to work at developing a common sense of what we hoped to do or become by living together. We hadn't established any rituals—like community projects, meals together, sharing music, or worship. Part of that may have been that the loss of Mark and Anne from our group meant that we had no real age diversity and the fact that none of us stepped into an active leadership role. Another part of it may have been our continuing and growing sense of alienation—from the church, from larger society—and our weariness from the intensity of it all.

This was further complicated by the dynamics put in play by Jeanne and me becoming a couple just as we were all moving into the apartments and trying to establish the collective. Jeanne had returned from her Guatemala trip in August, and we dove into developing our relationship. Our intense mutual interest in each other and the novelty of being able to sleep and live together meant we were primarily spending time with each other, most often to the exclusion of the others.

I am sure we were largely oblivious to the impact our relationship had on the group's formation. And on this particular afternoon, I felt nothing—no guilt, no worries, no frustrations—related to the myriad of issues and concerns I had been focused on all that summer and, really, for years now. There was nothing I was feeling that afternoon other than bliss: the absolute euphoria that comes with being completely enthralled, enchanted, and entwined with the human being you love.

* * *

The fall flew by and before I knew it, it was Christmastime, and I was back in Webster Groves to spend the holidays with my family. On the second morning of my visit, I found myself in the kitchen in the throes of a major argument with my mother. I had convinced myself that she would be relieved and appreciative, but instead she was furious with me. "Go tell your father about it—*he'll* be happy!" my mother shouted at me as she stormed out of the kitchen. I slunk down the basement stairs to my dad's office, where he was fiddling with his ham radio equipment.

"CQ, calling CQ, CQ," he was saying. "This is W0HKH beaming west from St. Louis, Missouri, calling CQ, CQ, W0HKH, W0 Henry King Henry calling CQ, over." With his headphones on and his attention focused on his transceiver, Dad took no notice of me. I moved to the side of his desk and waved. He held up one finger and continued to repeat his call signal. After apparently getting no response, he flicked a few switches and took off his headphones. "Paul-o! To what do I ascribe the honor of your presence? I thought you were off somewhere—"

"No, no. Just got up and was talking to Mom. You have many CTs this morning?" I pointed to the log lying open on the desk in front of him, where he recorded his contacts—CTs—with other amateur radio operators across the globe. Ham radio had been a part of his life since he was a teenager and—along with fishing—was one of his chief passions.

"Nah, I'm just fooling around," he said. "It's too early in the day for much action."

"Uh huh, well, I guess, well I came down to see if we could talk."

"Sure, sure. Pull that stool over. Now, what's going on? Is everything OK in Chicago, with that commune or whatever you and Joe are into there?"

"Yeah, yeah. No, it's about the draft, my draft status," I said.

"Oh, jeez, did something happen? The FBI? I've been worried that they'd put two and two together ever since they came to my office last year—"

"No, no, not them, nothing like that at least not yet. No, I wanted to tell you and Mom that I decided to go ahead and register. I mean, I did register, just a couple of weeks ago. I sent the draft board that covers my part of the Chicago area a letter. Here, I made a copy so that you could see it." I gave him a file folder. He opened it, took out the thin sheet of yellow onionskin paper that I had made the carbon copy on and began reading:

My name is Paul Kuehnert, my birthdate, June 17, 1952. Today I presented myself at your office to fulfill my legal obligation to register for the draft: one year and a half later than is required by the law. I would like to offer a brief explanation as to why I have registered late. This hopefully will avoid misunderstanding as much as possible.

For over 2 years now, I have felt strongly opposed to war and organized aggressive violence in any form. This belief is based in and stems from my Christian beliefs: I was raised in and am still a member of the Lutheran Church-Missouri Synod. At the time of my 18th birthday, I felt so strongly about this conscientious objection to war that I felt I could not support the military in any way or be a part of any institution that supplied men or arms for war efforts. Thus, I decided I could not and would not register.

I want to make clear the fact that my opposition to war is unchanged and unalterable. However, I no longer feel that I should or have to show that opposition by violating the Selective Service law. Therefore, I have registered, and I plan to file for a 1-0 classification in order to be congruent with my beliefs and yet stay within the law.

I know that this is a very brief explanation of my late registration, however, I do hope that it gives you a basic understanding of my reasons. I am certainly willing to make a personal appearance to explain myself further on this matter if you so desire. Thank you.

Sincerely,

Paul L. Kuehnert

Daddy looked up and held my eyes with his for a moment, his eyes welling up. "I'm surprised by this, Paul," he said. "I mean, this is what I have been saying to you from the start, so, well, I am relieved, too. But, is this what you really want? What you believe is right?"

I leaned back against the basement wall, feeling a little confused. Despite their support and acceptance, I thought my parents hadn't really been listening to me and my earlier arguments for draft resistance over the last two years. I thought that had just gone along somehow, maybe for the sake of family peace. But it seemed like each of them had internalized my arguments with the passage of time. Now they seemed to want to understand my apparent change of heart.

"Yeah, I think it is right for me now," I explained. "I mean, like I say in the letter, my opposition to the war and to the draft has not changed. It's just that I am not wanting to be taken out of my work for peace and for, well, I guess I would say, revolution. I need to be organizing, getting people to take actions together over the long haul that it will take to change this country. I would never go if I got drafted, but I've just gotta believe that non-registration puts a target on my back."

"So now you are being, what, *practical*?" he asked. The edge of sarcasm in his question was unmistakable and familiar. I felt my face begin to flush.

"I think it's more tactical, what works!" I said. "The movement has to be built for the long run and taking individual actions on the draft that most people can't or won't do, that just doesn't work for me anymore."

"Your conscience is not a tactic, though. You have been saying that for years now." He was smirking. Daddy liked nothing more than an argument—especially an argument he felt he was winning.

"OK, OK, look, you are right about conscience not being a tactic," I responded. "My conscience will not let me be part of this war, and I won't be. It's just that the last year-plus has taught me some things, mainly that to really stop the war we must move millions of people. Individual acts don't necessarily do that, for sure don't do that."

And so it went. Back and forth for hours, first with Daddy, and then with Mom. The arguments were reprised over the following days with each of them, and sometimes with both of them and my younger brothers around the dinner table. Mom argued vehemently that I should return to the resistance and publicly burn whatever the draft board sent me as a result of my registration. While she had little problem with my growing belief that truly transformative social change was needed in the United States and liked what we were doing by building an intentional community in the Austin neighborhood and in organizing tenants there, she did not believe that negated the need for individual, moral actions against the war and the draft. My father was worried about me becoming a socialist, as he saw it, and argued with both of us.

It all felt so familiar.

* * *

I wasn't expecting any calls. So, when my youngest brother, Steve, pounded on the bedroom door to wake me from a sound sleep at about 9:30 the morning after Christmas, I was none too happy.

"Get up, get up! You got a phone call!" Steve said.

"What the hell? I mean, who, what? Wait, what time is it?" I asked

"It's morning. And it's some girl. She didn't say her name. Anyway, she's out here waiting on your sleepy ass."

As I crawled out of bed, I heard him walk away from my door and up the hall to the phone. I couldn't make it out, but he apparently said something to the caller before I heard him bounding down the stairs. I opened my door and saw the phone, with the receiver hanging suspended from the dialing unit and swinging gently back and forth in a shortening arc. I grabbed the receiver and lifted it to my ear.

"Hello?"

"Hey, there! Merry Christmas!" Jeanne was speaking softly, almost whispering.

"Well, hey yourself, and Merry Christmas a day late. How are you? Where are you? Is everything OK?" I asked. The words came rushing out. I was so thrilled to hear Jeanne's voice and realized that I had been feeling a little low spending Christmas apart from her. We had talked about it a little and agreed that it made sense since neither set of our parents knew that we were even interested in each other romantically. They knew that we were living in the two apartments with other friends. But, whereas I had told my parents that this was the "Austin Collective,"—an intentional community with social, political and religious components to it—Jeanne had decided to present it to her parents as simple convenience and friendship, that she and Gail and Hildy were roommates, and Joe, Tedd and I were living across the hall. We sometimes shared supper and did social things together, she explained to them.

"I am at home, I mean, in Lombard, with my parents," she said. "Everything is OK. I just wanted to talk to you for a minute while all of them are out of the house. I have to be quick."

"Well, yeah, I mean, it's long distance and stuff. But, uh, I miss you, Jeanne. I didn't realize it would be hard to be away from you, but it is."

"I miss you too, but, well, that's not why I called." Jeanne paused. "Something came up, yesterday, well, last night, really."

I held my breath. I knew Jeanne had dated a guy in high school that was a couple of years older and was now, I thought, at Maryknoll Seminary. Maybe he had come up from Joliet for a Christmas visit and announced he was leaving the seminary? Man, if she was going to dump me now, on the phone, I wouldn't know what to do with myself. I exhaled, audibly.

"Are you there?" she asked. "I heard something, and I hope nobody picked up an extension."

"Yeah, yeah. No, it was me. So, what about last night?"

Jeanne explained that she had been talking with her parents late the night before when the conversation turned to her living arrangements and their concerns about her living in a 'changing neighborhood' in Chicago. In trying to assuage their concerns, she told them that I walked her to and from the el stop each day. Then, somehow, she said, one thing led to another and she ended up telling them that we were involved with each other and that it was a serious relationship. She concluded, saying: "I told them we wanted to get married!"

"What!? Holy shit! I mean, Jesus, Jeannie!"

"I know, I know. But, look, it just came out, OK? I mean, I couldn't say we want to live together, that would just freak them out. So, it just came into my head and I said it. Then, well, they were smiling and happy and stuff, but then they said, well, they barely met you, they hardly know you at all. They want you to come and spend New Year's here with us in Lombard."

"Well, I," I began, but I was distracted. The conversation went on for another couple of minutes as we talked over plans for me getting back to Chicago by New Year's Eve and then making my way to Lombard. Then she had to go—her family was arriving back home and she did not want to be on the phone when they came in the house.

I hung up the phone and walked back to my bedroom. My head was spinning. A few minutes ago, I had thought she was going to dump me on the phone. I was sure I was deeply in love with Jeanne. But, after three months of living together, I had felt unsure that the depth of my feelings was totally reciprocated. I took a deep breath.

I grabbed my jeans, shirt and underwear out of the suitcase sprawled open on the floor by my bed and walked down the hall again to the bathroom and closed the door. After relieving myself I flushed the toilet, closed the lid and sat down. I sat staring at the light coming through the frosted window above the bathtub, mesmerized. Playing the conversation I had just had with Jeanne back in my head. My brother's shout interrupted my train of thought.

"Hey, you done with the phone?"

"Yeah! All yours!"

I got up, put the plug in the drain and turned on the hot water. As the water rushed into the tub, I examined my face in the mirror: my hair, frizzy and curled, hung over my ears and down the back of my neck; my wispy goatee; my cheeks and forehead splotched in at least half a dozen places with acne; my black, horn-rimmed glasses and crossed left eye.

"Yeah, what a catch you are!" I told my reflection. I took out my toothbrush, loaded it with paste, and furiously brushed my teeth, taking a break to adjust the water temperature as the tub filled. I finished brushing my teeth, stripped and stepped into the steaming water, slowly sitting and easing myself back into a reclining position.

I smiled as I returned, now for the umpteenth time, to the phone conversation I had just had with Jeanne. I was sure that had to have been the weirdest quasi-marriage proposal any couple had ever had in all time. And, I realized, I had not even been thinking about marriage. I was perfectly happy living with her and living with our friends, trying to create a community, trying to build a movement for fundamental change, justice and peace. My focus had been on resolving my personal draft resistance dilemma around registration. I felt I had come to the right conclusion, although my arguments with my parents, especially my mother, made me unsure of myself. I had not yet heard from the draft board and had no idea what was really going to happen next. They could register and classify me 1-A or make me a conscientious objector, draft me, or maybe even refer me for prosecution to make an example of me; I didn't know. Even though what might happen next with the draft was now out of my hands, I had worked my way to a decision I felt was right and acted.

I let out a huge sigh, took a deep breath and slid my shoulders and head under the warm water. I held my breath until I couldn't stand the tightness in my chest and pushed myself up, splashing and gasping. I leaned back on the smooth porcelain again and let my breathing slow and become regular.

But, now. Now marriage. And marriage specifically to Jeanne. Part of me was so thrilled—a dream I wasn't aware that I really had now surfaced and was going to be fulfilled. Another part of me, though, was uneasy. In those early moments of this new possibility arising in my life, though, I pushed those feelings down. Deep down. Unlike my deliberate approach to deciding to resist the draft, and then, more recently, to stepping back from non-registration, , I had just agreed to go along with Jeanne and announce to her parents that we wanted to marry, even though we had spent only a few minutes talking about it on the phone. We had not talked about it with any close friends. I had not talked about it with my parents or Susie or Joe.

I wish now that I had called Jeanne back and said that we needed to talk first. That this was moving too fast and we needed to take some time to really talk through what we were going to be doing and committing ourselves to. That would have probably been hard to do and might have caused some difficult, even painful moments over the next several hours or days. Instead, it turned out, we deferred those difficult and painful moments into our future.

But in that moment, I slid down into the water. I closed my eyes, held my breath, and let the warm water wash over and hold me. I surfaced slowly, shampooed, rinsed, and washed the rest of my body. I toweled off and faced myself in the mirror again. This time I grinned widely and shook my head, thinking I was the luckiest 19-year-old man on the planet!

CHAPTER 8:
ANOTHER KIND OF COMMITMENT

Tommy had been doing this since before I was born. He wanted to make sure I knew that. And he found ways to remind me, each and every time we met up to go out and knock doors.

"Look. Everybody knows me," Tommy said. "They know I can help them out. Me standin' here with you at their door says everythin' they need to know about the party and McGovern. You just keep doin' the talkin' and don't worry about me not talkin'."

I had had the temerity to question Tommy about his support for Senator McGovern after our experience at the last house. There, an older white working-class guy—someone like Tommy—on the other side of the door had berated McGovern "… and all you fuckin' hippies!" for his antiwar stance. Tommy said nothing to the man, and my arguments got nowhere with him. He didn't slam the door in our faces, at least, but he wouldn't say how he was going to vote. As we walked along the sidewalk toward the next house, I put a minus sign next to his name on my list of voters in the precinct. I noticed Tommy put a plus next to his name, that of his wife and two others that had the same address and same last name. I asked him why and Tommy said "He's one of our guys. Always votes, him, the wife, the boys. Solid, lever A." "Solid lever A" or "no dancing in the booth" was party shorthand, I had learned, for voting a straight Democratic Party ticket.

Tommy would explain these things to me and then expected me to stop questioning him and get back to knocking on doors.

Tommy was the precinct captain for the 22nd Ward Democratic Party organization in the Austin neighborhood of Chicago. He was born in the hospital on Cicero Avenue and had lived in the neighborhood his whole life. He had always worked in the City of Chicago's Department of Streets and Sanitation. Or, at least that is who paid him. As far as I could tell, he worked for the Democratic Party full-time, out of the alderman's office. But, under Mayor Daley, working for the city and for the party were pretty much the same thing. What mattered was that Tommy delivered the votes by large margins in every election—and had been doing so since he became precinct captain in 1958.

In contrast, I was a complete neophyte in electoral politics. On a whim, Jeanne and I had stopped by the McGovern for President headquarters on West Chicago Avenue in late September. We agreed to help the campaign by working in our neighborhood, so they gave us a printed list of all precinct voters listed by block and trained us on the basics of canvassing. They loaded us down with McGovern for President flyers and encouraged us to stop over at the 22nd Ward Democratic campaign headquarters, which is where we met Tommy. I had been spending every weekend since walking the precinct and talking to voters with Tommy.

As I continued knocking on doors and saying the same things over and over again to the voters I met, I noticed once again that most of the people I was meeting in my new neighborhood were busy with their lives. They might have a practical question about city services or getting a job, but the urgency I still felt about ending the war—urgency that I had now shifted to beating Richard Nixon at the polls—was not a reality for most people. Sure, they said, they would vote for McGovern because "the mayor likes him, right Tommy? Oh, and can you guys do something about the streetlight right there? It's burned out, has been for weeks and nobody has come out."

We ticked off a few more houses, and then Tommy showed me where our polling place was going to be on North Mayfield. Since it was 10 days until the election, we planned to do some canvassing after work the following week and then, a final push on the weekend before Election Day. He reminded me to make sure and take Election Day off so that we could work together to get all our voters to the polls.

We shook hands, and I hurried toward Austin Boulevard. It had been a pleasantly warm day, but as the sun was setting the breeze had kicked up, reminding me it was late October in Chicago and winter was just around the corner. I bent my head into the wind and reflected on how I had come to be working at the grassroots of a political campaign for one of the two mainstream candidates for president when, less than a year before, I had been struggling with the question of how best to advance fundamental and radical change in the country. I went back and forth, sometimes thinking it was through individual acts of conscience and resistance and, at others, believing it had to be some form of collective organizing to change the power structure. Although I had somehow created this "either/or" choice for myself and ended up deciding to register for the draft after all, it struck me that if I had been asking the voters I was talking to about the choices my friends and I debated, they would have been puzzled at best.

I reached the corner of Chicago and Austin and waited for the light to change so I could walk the last few blocks to the big, yellow-brick court-yard building that we had moved into a few weeks ago. The tiny three-room walk-up Jeanne and I now shared was quite a change from the expansive, dozen rooms of the two apartments that had made up our Austin Collective. As the light changed and I crossed the street, I thought more about my evolution from draft resister to McGovern campaign worker. Early in March, my local draft board had responded to my letter and late registration by sending me a 1-A draft card. I responded, in turn, with my application for conscientious objector status, which was quickly rejected. So I was still 1-A, but, in the meantime, President Nixon had instituted a draft lottery, and I had drawn a high number. The combination of my high number and the new "Vietnamization" of the war—withdrawing U.S. troops and rapidly increasing South Vietnamese troops while continuing ferocious U.S. bombing raids across Vietnam, Laos, and Cambodia—meant that the likelihood of my being drafted was almost zero[4]. By the time my Walther League contract ended in July 1972 I felt that everything I was doing was futile. I found no clear, compelling analysis of what was happening, either within the larger antiwar movement or even in our work as Walther League in our denomination or in the church community writ large. I had looked further to the left for answers, seriously studying Marxism, labor history and the Chinese revolution with the *Peoples' Voice* group. But by the end of our year in the Austin Collective, I was completely alienated by a "heart-to-heart" that their leader, Al, had with me, warning me not to marry Jeanne shortly before our wedding. Jeanne had resolutely refused to join in the collective study groups, and Al relayed the story of another friend who had committed suicide after his wife refused to participate in study groups. I remember thinking at the time that it was the most insensitive, crazy thing to tell me—and I never took another thing he had to say seriously.

I turned into our courtyard and looked up to see the light shining out of the bay windows of our third-floor apartment. I shook my head quickly to clear out the thoughts of Al, the war, Tommy, and the precinct. I pushed open our entrance door, turned my key in the door to the stairs and rushed up, two stairs at a time, eager to see what the evening held in store for Jeanne and me.

* * *

We were so excited and hopeful on Election Day. The McGovern campaign notified us that our precinct had been chosen by NBC as one of the "national indicator" precincts that they would be tracking on election

---

4. What I didn't fully understand then—and only learned in much more detail later—was that this policy change was a strategic response to the tenacious Vietnamese people and their military allies, as well as the impact I and others had indeed had through the mass mobilizations of antiwar protesters, hundreds of thousands of non-registrants for the draft#, thousands of noncooperative U.S. soldiers, sailors, and Marines. For more, see *Chance and Circumstance* and *The War Within*.

night to predict the outcome. With this news in mind, we worked the precinct with Tommy and his assistants and got out every vote that we could. We were able to stay behind after the polls were closed and watch as the official poll workers and watchers opened the voting machines and tallied the vote from the precinct. We were thrilled when not only McGovern won the precinct with a huge vote total, but that the notorious Edward Hanrahan, Democratic State's Attorney and architect of the police raid that murdered Black Panther leader Fred Hampton three years earlier, had gone down to defeat in our precinct[5]. Jeanne and I were elated, while Tommy and his assistants saw Hanrahan's loss as the bigger news and were visibly shaken by the clear fact that Democratic voters in their precinct had asserted their independence and "split their tickets" by voting for a Republican candidate for State's Attorney. While they went off to drown their sorrows and contemplate their futures, we rushed down Chicago Avenue to McGovern headquarters, expecting a long, but ultimately satisfying, night watching the returns roll in with our fellow McGovernites.

Instead, we walked into a small crowd with tear-stained faces. Senator McGovern was on TV giving his concession speech we came in. Jeanne immediately burst into tears, as we watched in disbelief as the man who we were so certain the American people would listen to and vote for told us that our hopes had been misplaced. The scale of his defeat was only emerging, but the early concession was a telltale sign of what the eventual outcome would be. We walked home a little later, silent and dazed.

Over the following days and weeks we processed the new reality that had been ushered in by Nixon's historic landslide victory. One Saturday in early December we headed a few blocks down Austin to have dinner with Peggy Curran and Nathan Gardels who, like us, had recently been married. Nathan and Peggy had spent most of the summer and fall working on the Indochina Peace Campaign (IPC) organized by Tom Hayden and Jane

---

5. Hanrahan was defeated in his bid to be re-elected that year for States Attorney in Cook County, the first sign of significant cracks in the democratic machine's absolute power under then Mayor Richard J. Daley.

Fonda. We were eager to catch up and compare experiences of different approaches to election campaigns as a strategy to stop the war.

What stuck with me most from our long conversation that evening, though, was Nathan's description of the "dirty tricks" that the IPC had been subjected to over the course of the fall. At the time, the true dimensions of the Watergate break-in and cover-up were only beginning to come to light. The detailed accounts of harassment, break-ins, thefts of IPC records, and counter-IPC campaign flyers filled with fiction and outright lies all seemed hard to fathom. Yet, IPC staff had thoroughly documented all the incidents and traced much of the operations and financing of the operations against them to Nixon's Committee to Re-Elect the President (CRP) Nathan, talented journalist that he was, would assemble this material into a report that the IPC released the next year as the true dimensions of Watergate and its implications began to unfold.

After listening to Peggy and Nathan's frightening stories of harassment and intimidation, and then reflecting together on the enormity of Nixon's victory—combined with what seemed to be the fizzling out of the mass antiwar movement now that only 27,000 U.S. troops were left in Vietnam and the draft being eliminated in mid-1973—I felt overwhelmed, sad, even listless. While jokingly referring to the amount of wine I had drunk as being the reason I didn't feel like getting up off the couch and walking home, at that moment, I really had no energy. For the first time in my life I had a deep visceral sense of dread and foreboding. I remember thinking: "Oh, this is depression starting. This is what Daddy gets."

That thought—not Jeanne's exasperation or Nathan's cajoling—got me off the couch, into my coat and out into the cold, headed home.

* * *

Things only got worse. A few days before Christmas, Nixon launched the most massive bombing campaign of the war so far, targeting Hanoi and Haiphong, and without regard to the impact on civilians. Eyewitness accounts of the terror and the impact—for example, the destruction of Bach Mai Hospital in Hanoi—circulated rapidly through the news media and brought the slumbering antiwar movement back into the streets.

And we were part of the no-longer-slumbering movement, spending a cold early January Saturday morning at a march down Michigan Avenue culminating in a rally numbering in the thousands outside the Federal building in Chicago. Jeanne's mother had joined us in what was her first antiwar rally and really got into the chant of "NIXON, YOU LIAR, SIGN THE CEASE FIRE!" I remember thinking that I had never talked with her about my draft resistance and wondered what she would think. Although the non-registration was in the past, I was still worried about being drafted or even arrested and tried in court as some sort of punishment for my late registration and my advocacy of non-cooperation with the draft. I didn't put anything past this president and his loyal followers, thinking specifically about Nathan's and Peggy's tales of the CRP's strategy of harassment and spying. If you were going to start the war up again with a vengeance, why not go after and try to take out as many antiwar activists as possible, I thought as chills ran up my spine. I shivered and my teeth started chattering. Jeanne noticed and grabbed me.

"Don't just stand there! Move around! You'll warm up!" she said. I grinned and began jumping up and down and making exaggerated clenched fist salutes in time with the chanting crowd.

"Nixon, YOU LIAR! Sign the ceasefire!"

The phone kept ringing. Ringing. It was my day off, a Thursday, and I was determined to sleep in. Jeanne was already at work, and Tedd and I had stayed out late the night before.

"Damn! Tedd! I almost forgot," I mumbled to my pillow, turned over, and threw off the covers. Tedd was visiting us from St. Louis and sleeping on the couch in the living room. Or trying to, I thought, as the phone was picked up in mid-ring.

"Hello?" Tedd was almost whispering. "No. Yes. He's here. Let me go find him."

I had pulled on my jeans and was stumbling out into the little dining area off the kitchen. The phone was mounted on the wall, and Tedd held his hand over the mouthpiece of the receiver as he stood near the kitchen sink. He turned and held the phone out toward me. "Some guy. He didn't say what he wanted, just asked for you."

"Sorry, man. I shoulda got it," I apologized. "Sorry to wake you."

"That's OK. I'll make some coffee." He handed over the phone and ducked under the long coiled extension cord that stretched from the phone's handset to the wall in order to get to the shelves and the coffee. I stretched the cord out as I walked away from the kitchen and into the alcove outside the bathroom. At that moment, I felt how full my bladder was, but held off going into the bathroom with the phone. Even though the cord would reach, I thought it would be pretty rude. Still, I thought, gotta make this short, whoever this guy is.

"Hello?" I said.

"Yes. Am I speaking with Paul, uhmm, Cooner?"

"Kuehnert, yes!" I snapped at the typical mispronunciation of my name. I really wanted to pee. Now. "Who is this and what can I do for you?"

"Yes. Kuehnert. Yes. This is Bill Hawkins, special agent Bill Hawkins, of the Federal Bureau of Investigation. Now, no need to be alarmed. I need your help." I grabbed the back of a chair from the dining room table, pulled it out, and sat down. Tedd looked over at me and raised his eyebrows, mouthing "What?" I just shook my head.

"I see. What exactly do you want?" I asked.

"Well, Mr. Cooner, I mean, Kuehnert, your name has come up in a case I am working on," the agent said. "It'd be helpful if I could come over and talk to you. Are you there at 634 North Austin, Apartment 3-E? I can come over right away so I don't take up too much of your time on your day off."

"My what? I mean, it sounds—I mean, whatever. Why not, I guess," I said

"OK, like I said, nothing to worry about," he replied. "See you soon."

I got up and hung up the phone. Tedd was looking at me intently, waiting for an explanation. "Who—?"

"Sorry, man, Really gotta piss. Bad." I went to the bathroom, shut the door and finally relieved myself. As I did, I could feel my heart racing. This was it! They were coming for me. I just knew it. As I washed my hands, I took a few deep breaths and pulled myself together. I went out to talk to Tedd, who was busy straightening up the living room and explained who had called and what they wanted. He immediately said, "Do you think it's about the draft?"

Tedd had given voice to my major fear. He and I and Joe had talked for hours about it when I was making my decision to register, so I guess it shouldn't have been a surprise to me. Still, it just shook me to hear another person say it. It was real. They were finally coming after me.

"It's weird, yeah," I said. "What the guy said on the phone was it wasn't about me or something. Made it sound like something else, but, I mean, what else could it be? We speculated about what the agents were up to for another few minutes and then decided that we might as well make breakfast. Tedd took a quick shower while I made more coffee and rooted around to find cereal, yogurt, and toast. I thought about calling Jeanne as the coffee was percolating but decided against bothering her at work until I knew more about what the FBI wanted to me. We ate and drank coffee, and I chain-smoked. The minutes crawled by.

The doorbell buzzed. I jumped out of my chair and pushed the buzzer to unlock the electronic lock of the stairway door.

"Come on up!" I shouted into the speaker that connected to one in the lobby. I opened our door and stepped out onto the carpeted stairway and landing that we shared with our neighbors across the hall. I heard the door open and peered into the space between the railings to see the two men I assumed were Federal agents climbing the stairs. I turned back into the living room, leaving the door open. My heart raced as I faced the doorway and listened to their progress up the creaking stairs. I pushed my glasses up and straightened them and took a deep breath as I rubbed my damp palms against the back of my jeans. I could sense Tedd standing behind me in the door to the dining room.

Then they were there. Two middle-aged white men in dark overcoats, suits, and ties. They paused at the open door and flashed their badges. "Hawkins and Fisher. FBI. Can we come in?" one of them said.

I stepped toward them. "Let me see the badges up close, please." I looked closely at the ID cards and the gold badges. Everything seemed to be legit. "Yeah, yeah. Come in, I guess." I stepped back to the center of the living room.

They entered the room and closed the door. Tedd stayed in the dining room doorway. Agent Hawkins nodded toward me. "Are you Paul COONert?" he asked.

"Yes, but I say KEY-nert."

"And who is this?" Agent Hawkins nodded toward Tedd as his partner slowly moved in Tedd's direction.

"Oh, just a friend," I said. "He was here having coffee when you called and I asked him to stay."

"Yeah? And what is your name, friend?" Hawkins asked. Tedd started to speak and I interrupted.

"I thought you wanted to talk with me about something? He's just here, visiting me."

Tedd spoke up. "No, Paul, it's OK. I don't mind. I'm Tedd and I am Paul's friend, like he said."

"Thanks, Tedd," Agent Hawkins said. "Now, do you guys mind if we sit down? This will just take a few minutes."

We shuffled around and found seats. Tedd and I sat next to each other on the couch while Agent Hawkins took the overstuffed armchair. Agent Fisher wandered into the dining room and came back with a chair from the dining set and sat down across the room from Hawkins. He pulled out a small notebook and a pen.

"Now, Tedd, you live around here too?" Agent Hawkins asked.

"No, I—"

"Really, Tedd," I interrupted him. "This doesn't have to involve you, man. Agent Hawkins, he is my friend and that's it."

"Last name?" Fisher spoke for the first time.

"Mayer," Tedd said.

"OK, Paul, where is your wife today?"

"What? I mean, at work, but you said on the phone you just had a question for me about somebody else, not me. I have to ask you to get to the point." I could hear that my voice sounded shaky, but I was beginning to get angry. I took a deep breath and looked Hawkins in the eye.

"OK, look," Hawkins said. "This is a routine investigation and you need to just cooperate, and answer the questions, OK?"

"Routine investigation, OK," I said. "What exactly are you investigating?"

"Look, here's the thing. Your name was found in an address book that came into our possession. It's an address book of a member of the Revolutionary Union[6]. We want to know why your name would be in that address book?"

6. The Revolutionary Union (RU) was a national Marxist group that had come out of a split of the SDS or Students for a Democratic Society in 1969. *Peoples' Voice* was the paper that RU published in Chicago.

"What? I have no idea."

"But you know the Revolutionary Union?" asked Hawkins. "You know their members in the area?" I could see where this was going and I didn't like it. Still, I was relieved that—at least so far—nothing was coming up about the draft. At the same time, I was experiencing the reason why lawyers in the movement admonished us to never agree to an interview with the FBI unless you had to—because of an actual criminal investigation—and you had a lawyer present.

"Look," I said. "When you called, I thought there was something with a missing person or something, the way you talked. This is just a fishing expedition for you guys."

"Paul, are you a member of the RU?" I must have looked shocked, although I was trying to maintain a neutral face. "I mean, we know we've seen you around, selling the paper, but it's been a while." I shook my head and stood up. I couldn't believe it, but it was clear they had *Peoples' Voice* under surveillance or maybe they had someone inside. Or worse, since I had really stopped hanging out and working with the collective since before I got married, maybe the Feds were going to try to use me now. I stood up.

"The interview is over. I have nothing else to say to you." I walked toward the door, and Agent Hawkins got up and stepped toward me.

"Look, son," he said. "These Revolutionary Union people are not good people. They are up to no good. Think it over and call me if you have more to say." He held his card out to me. I stood, holding the door open and looking past Hawkins, into the hallway. He shrugged, pocketed his card and walked out the door. Fisher followed. I watched them go down the stairs, heard the door open and then I rushed over to the living room windows overlooking the courtyard and watched the agents trudge away.

"JESUS H. CHRIST! THOSE FUCKERS!" I shouted at Tedd.

"I fuckin' can't believe it!" Tedd said.

"They stole somebody's address book," I shouted, "and now they are trying to use it to construct a list of members of RU, those fucks! I mean, I don't really care for Al and those guys anymore, but, these fuckin' Feds!" We spent the rest of the morning going over the interview: who said what, how it was said, what we should have said or done and didn't, what we did do right, and what it all meant. We talked about calling Al and giving him a heads up, but rejected the idea, since neither of us wanted to get caught up in the *Peoples' Voice* politics and drama again. When Jeanne came home from work, we re-hashed it all.

Later that night, as I crawled into bed and snuggled up to a sleeping Jeanne, I played through my mental tape of the FBI agents' visit one more time. I was irritated with myself for agreeing to talk with them and knew they had gotten some information from me just because I let them into my home. Still, I had gotten some information too: y draft resistance and advocacy did not appear to be on the FBI's radar. It was puzzling to me, since I had to believe that some of the church conservatives who disliked and disagreed with my actions and worked so actively to ostracize the Walther League would have reported me to law enforcement. But now, over the space of nearly three years, my father had been investigated for associating with the Black Panthers, I had been arrested in D.C., and now I was being investigated for associating with the Revolutionary Union. Through all these incidents with law enforcement, no one had asked me any draft-related questions, nor apparently, launched an investigation of any kind. And although I didn't know it then, when I obtained portions of my FBI file some four years later under the Freedom of Information Act, the contents of the file confirmed the conclusion I reached that night: that they either didn't know about, or didn't care about, my act of draft resistance.

That night, though, I reached the conclusion that, really and truly, the Feds were not after me. I marveled at the irony of it all: My belief that being a non-registrant left me vulnerable to harassment, arrest and being sidelined and so, I decided to register. After committing a couple of felonies that I was not being investigated for, I was now being investigated and harassed for exercising what were supposedly constitutionally protected rights to freedom of association and speech.

Jeanne stirred. I realized I was disturbing her sleep. I let go of her and turned away, staring at the shadowy display made by the lights from the courtyard below coming through the imperfectly closed shades. I felt that, somehow, I had finished a chapter in my life that day. I was done worrying about draft resistance and going to jail. I had to look forward and not back.

In the past few months, I had taken some tentative steps toward shaping my future by applying to three community college nursing programs in the area. I had been told by all three that I had to complete college-level chemistry before I would be admitted. And so, I was now taking chemistry at one of the Chicago City Colleges, Wilbur Wright, a few miles from our apartment. I was finding chemistry to be pretty interesting and engaging, not at all what I remembered from high school. I hoped to do well in chemistry, get admitted to one of the programs, and be able to start school in the fall. Jeanne was going back to school too, at University of Illinois-Chicago, where she had already taken several courses during her days on the Walther League staff.

So, there was school. But, what else? Work? Having children? How would I make a difference? I had no idea. For so long my faith had defined me; it had shaped what I did and how I made sense of the world. But, in the last year of my work in the church, I had lost my faith. I told myself and everyone who would listen that this was due to my church's harsh and, I felt, hypocritical, treatment of the Walther League. And so, community organizing to stop the war and for fundamental social change took up the space and energy in my life that my faith had filled.

But now, I knew I wanted to take a break from organizing and activism as a way of life. I knew I wanted to go to school and find a way to do some good for people every day while making a living. I knew that I wanted to have a meaningful, loving relationship with Jeanne. And I knew I wanted us to work with others to change the world for the better.

I finally fell asleep that night after wrestling round and round with these questions. I awoke to the alarm in the gray light of the early winter morning, feeling more tired than when I had gone to bed. As I walked across the street to West Suburban Hospital to begin my shift taking patients to and from the operating room, my questions about the future surfaced again. They spent the day with me.

As they would, I found, until they were replaced by partial answers. And then, new questions. It's been that way pretty much every morning since.

EPILOGUE

Fifteen years ago, in a leadership seminar, the group of executive nurse leaders I was in was given crayons and paper. We were then given 10 minutes to create an image that told the story of our leadership journey. While my colleagues were busy drawing spiral-shaped pathways, elaborate multi-storied structures, and creatively illustrated maps, I sat for a few minutes puzzling out what I could draw. I have always felt like my artistic abilities had never grown beyond the stick figures I mastered in kindergarten. So, part of my hesitancy was fear of being embarrassed. Part was just driven by who I am: I like to think about things—sometimes for quite a while and from every angle—before I make my move.

I settled on the idea, grabbed a black crayon and quickly colored the whole sheet solid black. Maybe it was my worry about embarrassing myself, but I thought I detected some raised eyebrows from colleagues at my table. We were, of course, a very competitive group of overachievers and were furtively keeping an eye on each other's work as we labored over our drawings.

After scribbling the paper as black as I could in a couple of minutes, I grabbed a yellow crayon and started making dots and small circles randomly across, up and down the entire paper. Just as time was being called for the exercise, I sketched in a few very light lines between a dozen or so of the points and circles of various sizes, creating a faintly outlined pattern. We were then paired up with another nurse and given a few minutes each to explain what we had created and how it illustrated our leadership journey.

My concept, I explained to my colleague, Cheri, was that our lives begin as a random event in a universe of possibility: The black sky populated by stars, planets, and galaxies. Our circumstances—parents, hometown, class, race, gender—begin to shape our life journey, a journey that is further shaped by choices made for us and choices we make. Often, at the time we are making choices, particularly in our teen and adult years, it may seem that we are doing things randomly. Or we may think that we have—and are executing—a master plan. But unexpected things happen. Our life course changes in ways we would not have predicted.

Only by reflecting on what we have experienced might we begin to see a pattern or patterns. We see constellations—my lightly traced lines in the vastness—where others see only randomly occurring points of light.

Then, I pointed to a bright star in my sky and named it as the start of my leadership journey. I shared a couple of my stories from the Chicago Youth Leadership Institute in 1969 and where it led—through some zigs and zags, ups and downs—in my night sky. It was the first time in a long time that I had thought about my early days as a church youth leader, organizer and rebel. It was also the first time I had deliberately and consciously connected my professional self and the leadership roles I aspired to with my experiences as a young man in the movement.

At that 2004 workshop, I made a mental note to reflect on the connections and my leadership journey, and I have, a little here and a little there, over the years. This memoir is the product of some of that reflection. I am so privileged, and so deeply grateful, to have had the time, space, support, and encouragement from so many good friends and family members while going through the multi-year process of creating this book. I would like to express my thanks to a few key people who have made it possible.

First, I must thank my daughter, Stephanie. She is an awesome and accomplished writer. A few years ago, I went to her with the idea of a story of writing the story of Great Uncle Paul's act of resistance in 1917 and connecting it with mine in 1970. She listened patiently and then said:

"Nope. It's your story. *You* have to write it!" And she has encouraged me ever since. She also referred me to a colleague of hers, Theo Nestor, who became my writing coach and helped me get started on my learning journey about being serious about my writing and the art of writing memoir. Other friends, writers, and memoirists who have patiently reviewed my writing, made comments and suggestions, and pushed me to go on were David Stone, Toby Hollander, David Myers, and Beth Toner. I particularly want to thank Beth who worked with me closely as an editor as I finalized this manuscript.

I also need to thank dear friends Patricia Krause and Frieda Hamilton Fox who saw something in me back in 1968 and 1969. Pat and Frieda each challenged and supported me to develop and stay true to what I understood to be my conscience. Darrell Hoemann met me in first grade and never held that against me. Instead, he became my good friend in high school, and we shared a few "illegal smile[s]," as John Prine famously sang. Darrell introduced me to Joe Warnhoff and the rest, as they say, is history. Thank you, Joe and Darrell, both for all the serious talks and your refusal to take me seriously all the times I was way too serious. You each have been steadfast and amazing friends over all these years.

My sons, Dan and Evan, and my nephew, Corey Pattison, have tolerated my storytelling for many years and have even encouraged it with their questions. I thank them for their love and their own commitments to living lives that make a difference to our human community. My sisters—Judy and Susie—and my brothers—David and Steve—mean the world to me. They, along with our parents, shaped a family that helped shape me, test me, and always supported me. This book is dedicated to Susie, who was closest to me in age and was my soulmate when we were teenagers (except for when we hated each other!). My abiding regret is that she died before I conceived of this book. It would have been so much fun to have reflected on our experiences then, and what they led to. Nonetheless, she was with me all along the way.

Finally, my biggest thanks are saved for my wife, and the love of my life, Judith. I would not have completed this without her encouragement from day one, her thoughtful comments and suggestions along the way, and her willingness to share me with this project and all that it entailed.

Paul Kuehnert

December 2020